Measuring and Motivating Maintenance Programmers

Jerome B. Landsbaum
Certified Quality Analyst

Robert L. Glass
Computing Trends

Prentice Hall
Englewood Cliffs, NJ 07632

Library of Congress Cataloging-in-Publication Data

Landsbaum, Jerome B.
    Measuring and motivating maintenance engineers / Jerome B.
Landsbaum and Robert L. Glass.
        p.   cm.
    Includes bibliographical references (p.   ) and index.
    ISBN 0-13-567827-7
    1. Software maintenance--Management.   I. Glass, Robert L., 1932-
. II. Title.
QA76.76.S64L36   1992
005.1'6'0683--dc20   92-5956
                                                                  CIP

Editorial/production supervision
   and interior design: *Brendan M. Stewart*
Prepress buyer: *Mary McCartney*
Manufacturing buyer: *Susan Brunke*
Acquisitions editor: *Paul Becker*
Cover illustration: *P. Edward Presson*

© 1992 by Prentice-Hall, Inc.
A Simon & Schuster Company
Englewood Cliffs, New Jersey 07632

NOTE ON THE COVER: The struggling figure on the cover is based on a sculpture from antiquity of Laocoon struggling with serpents. According to Greek legend, Laocoon was a priest of Apollo at Troy who warned the Trojans against the ploy of the Trojan horse and, with his two sons, was killed by serpents sent by the Gods. On the cover, the serpents that entwined the struggling Laocoon have been transformed into plumbing that must be maintained despite the complexity introduced by many patches, changes, and new features added over the years. Properly managed, this struggle can be won.

The publisher offers discounts on this book when ordered in bulk quantities. For more information, write: Special Sales/Professional Marketing, Prentice Hall, Professional & Technical Reference Division, Englewood Cliffs, NJ 07632.

Printed in the United States of America
10 9 8 7 6 5 4 3 2 1

ISBN 0-13-567827-7

Prentice-Hall International (UK) Limited, *London*
Prentice-Hall of Australia Pty. Limited, *Sydney*
Prentice-Hall Canada Inc., *Toronto*
Prentice-Hall Hispanoamericana, S.A., *Mexico*
Prentice-Hall of India Private Limited, *New Delhi*
Prentice-Hall of Japan, Inc., *Tokyo*
Simon & Schuster Asia Pte. Ltd., *Singapore*
Editora Prentice-Hall do Brasil, Ltda., *Rio de Janeiro*

To Elaine

Contents

Preface

It's an old axiom that everyone talks about the weather, but no one ever does anything about it. Software maintenance, strangely, is much the reverse of this. While mind-boggling quantities of effort are expended on it, relatively little is written or spoken about it.

The data on maintenance are clear. An extensive and constantly increasing percentage of information systems resources is spent on it. Some companies no longer develop new software at all, as their entire software budget is consumed by maintenance. It's not that maintenance is necessarily a Pac Man gone mad, gobbling up all of the development resources; but for some companies at least, all the business problems that can be solved by a computer have been solved. As a result, some people are "doing something about" software maintenance because, as software people, that is the business they find themselves in.

The fact that people don't talk about maintenance much, given all of that, is strange. But if you look at the field of software from the point of view of

- academic sources
- papers published in the literature
- methodologies
- CASE tools
- guru pronouncements
- and even published books (!)

you would begin to suspect that software maintenance, in fact, hardly exists at all. The number of announcements and pronouncements about maintenance has increased over the years, but the volume has hardly kept pace with the increase in time and effort spent on doing maintenance.

In this book I would like to help begin to turn that tide. The company for which I work, Monsanto, has done a great deal of software maintenance. For many years we have discussed approaches to maintenance improvement, but more important, we have done much about it. This book tells the story of what we did and how we did it.

Most of the literature I have researched suggests ways to avoid maintenance problems by doing a better job in development. The experts describe the problems in exquisite detail but propose solutions only in vague platitudes. Furthermore, much of this literature includes considerable quantities of mathematical formulation and theoretical jargon (and sometimes even Latin!). As a programmer, systems analyst, and manager, a lot of this is Greek to me (including the Latin).

And for the most part, they do not tell you what to do if you already have a maintenance problem. What if most of the work in your shop is correcting and modifying existing programs and systems? What if you are currently having maintenance problems with a large inventory of programs? In the Central Information Systems Support Group at Monsanto, we had to come up with the answers to these questions. These answers are reported in this book.

We in data processing generally believe that our productivity and quality have been improving constantly since our business began, and that the rate of improvement has been accelerating. (I am not sure that anyone but us believes this.) I believe the things we did at Monsanto accelerated our rate of improvement well beyond the average.

In *Software Productivity*, published in 1983, Harlan Mills contends that there is a 10-to-1 productivity differential between the best and worst programmers. He further contends that this differential exists between the best and worst software organizations. There is no averaging effect because, *like college football teams, the shops with the best reputations attract the best programmers.* We tried to capitalize on this in our shop.

Data processing is a very new business, and measuring ourselves in data processing is even newer. The oldest written record of this activity I can find is from the late 1960s, and it's still pretty skimpy until the mid-to-late 1970s. Why then do we not have more on the subject? According to Peter Drucker, twenty years is the lead time for ideas. "Anything new is practiced at first only by a very small number of people. They find it useful. They do not keep it a secret, but nobody is greatly interested. . . . Twenty years later this becomes the great blinding insight to which everybody rushes."

The underlying questions in this book would never have been asked, and the answers it provides could never have been identified, without the considerable effort and strong commitment of a number of people in the Monsanto Central Management Information Systems Department. Hal White and Lou Malich got this book started when they involved me in Development Technology, and gave me the freedom to look for the answers. It is a terrible sorrow to me that neither Hal nor Lou have lived to see this book published. Both died of heart attacks; Hal a year before his fiftieth birthday, and Lou a year after his.

But this book could never have been written without Bob Adams, who provided the direction and leadership for most of the activities described here, and who had faith in my ability to contribute to those activities. Also important are Russ Sprague, who gave Bob the freedom to do them, and the others in the deparment who encouraged my work.

—Jerome B. Landsbaum

One of the fringe benefits of reviewing book manuscripts for Prentice-Hall is that every once in a while I come across a gem of a manuscript lacking only a little polish to become a gem of a book. That is how I first encountered this material written by Jerome Landsbaum.

I was impressed. Landsbaum writes with knowledge, with skill, but more to the point he writes with the confidence and fire of someone who has done what he is writing about, and who cares about what he has done. Too many authors in the field of computing and software are wanna-bees, people who lecture us about how to do things that they have never really done in practice.

Equally important, Landsbaum had written about software maintenance. Too little has been written about maintenance, a topic that is rapidly growing in importance as the years go by. There is a hunger among practitioners for solid, practice-based knowledge of software maintenance, and Landsbaum's manuscript looked like a meal to satisfy that hunger.

A year after reviewing the manuscript, I discovered that it was stalled for lack of author time. I volunteered to leap in, supplying the needed time and some of the polishing of that gem I mentioned earlier. The result is, I think, a significant book on software maintenance. The experiences and the wording of most of the book are Jerome Landsbaum's. I hope perhaps the gem shines a little brighter because of my contributions.

I recommend this book to anyone who cares about software and its maintenance:

- those who *do* maintenance
- those who manage maintenance
- high-level managers whose responsibilities include anything to do with software
- academics who teach software courses
- researchers who are exploring software and its maintenance

—Robert L. Glass

1

Background

1.1 PURPOSE OF THIS BOOK

The purpose of any book is, of course, to impart information. It is the particular intent of this book to describe management techniques to improve the performance of software maintenance personnel. It states not only *what* to do to accomplish this objective, but *how* to do it. It is a practical guide for managers of software maintenance groups, and is based on the actual experiences of the first author.

More specifically, the book covers measurement, performance, quality, productivity, management, and motivation. Therefore, having a common understanding of these concepts is imperative. This understanding is especially important in the case of quality, as there has been considerable disagreement on the definition of quality in the last several years.

In the field of software maintenance, it would be wonderful if there were "one true way to do the job." Then in this book we could share with you that one way, and you at your information systems shop could put in place all the wonderful things we did at Monsanto. But that approach simply won't work. Institutions differ. Applications differ. People differ.

There are too many choices of actions to take, too many different situations. You will find many choices of metrics to try and actions to take throughout this book. We have tried to indicate which ones worked for us. It is up to you to decide which ones, if any, to try in your situation.

A key premise of this book is that for people to grow and succeed, they must be given the opportunity to fail. According to Tom DeMarco in *Controlling Software Projects: Management, Measurement, & Estimation,* "The only unforgivable failure is the failure to learn from past failure." If as a manager you cannot accept an occasional failure as part of the investment you must make in the growth of your staff, don't waste your time reading this book.

Finally, implementing the changes recommended here requires going against tradition. To succeed, you must be willing to do this.

1.2 INTRODUCTION

Most of this book focuses on what we did about software maintenance at Monsanto, and the reasons for it. But for this to make sense to anyone from outside of this enterprise, it is important to describe our organizational constructs.

The department called Central Information Systems Support (CISS) had responsibility for information systems that were operated for corporate staff departments, or multiple operating units. This department was "Central" because each operating unit had its own information systems group. It had 55 people divided into five functional areas.

CISS was and is primarily a COBOL shop, using structured design and coding techniques, with a significant amount of on-line systems and programs. Clients are charged back for services, but it is very rare that any code written in this shop is sold outside of Monsanto. Support of these systems requires a very small amount of travel.

We knew we could not make improvements in systems maintenance in a vacuum. We realized that a clear top-level picture was needed of everything we were responsible for, taking into account, of course, Monsanto's overall business goals. To be effective, the picture would have to go beyond just being a study of what was; it would have to be a description of what would be. We laid out our plan of attack:

1. Understand the business situation.
2. Establish goals and directions.
3. Take action.
4. Evaluate the results.

Clearly, understanding the situation was our first and biggest task, and it was obvious even at the outset that there were substantial internal and external pressures to be considered. These are discussed shortly.

To establish a foundation of knowledge, we asked: What were others doing in measurement? In management? In motivation? And, in fact, in software quality and productivity? These questions were not unique; what was unique was that we had the opportunity to delve deeply into historic answers to these questions.

We looked at books, journal articles, and book reviews. We attended seminars, listened to audio tapes, and talked to university people. We conducted internal surveys. (The bibliography summarizes our research.)

We looked at environmental factors, such as physical layout, technology, and organization. We looked at the job itself to see how it was affecting performance. And we looked at the attitudes and internal psychological factors that motivate people.

Internal Pressure

What we first found inside our organization was difficult to accept but undeniable. Each of our project groups had staked out its own turf, dug foxholes, and built bunkers. Everyone was totally in favor of consistency, *as long as it turned out to be the way they were already doing it.* This attitude created our own internal pressure. The competition was counterproductive, leading to subtle, covert, stonewalling.

Tearing down bunkers such as these is not easy and requires continuous effort. But the best way we found to minimize the problem was by simply exposing it to the people involved. The old-style management practiced here was an informal system based on opinion, distrust, and promises. We needed to move away from this to a new management style based on facts, respect, accountability, and performance. The staff was in agreement with this assessment. Had we read Peter Drucker before we investigated, we would not have been so surprised. He says that analysis of a business always shows it to be in worse shape than originally expected.

External Pressure

Every business is subjected to varying degrees of pressure to maintain, alter, and/or improve its products, services, and profitability. In order to survive as a viable organization, the business must adapt to the changing conditions. Because we are so driven by technology and the needs of the corporation, management of this function is tantamount to the management of constant change. Following is a description of some of the forces impacting this function and limiting the options at Monsanto.

1. *Corporate Policy.* There are frequent changes in corporate organization, including operating units and staff departments. It is up to us to implement all of these changes in the corporate computer systems. And when we are decentralized, "new" development disappears. We become totally a "support" shop, that is, maintaining and/or improving existing function, and adding small amounts of new function, but not adding new systems. That function goes to the newly decentralized operating units.

Further, not adding new systems implies not adding new clients. Therefore, the clients we deal with today have been using computer systems for much longer than many of our programmers. Their level of sophistication has increased dramatically over the years, and this requires us to improve our products and services in order to keep them satisfied.

2. *Law and Government Regulations.* Changes in law and regulations have a number of effects on us. These occur primarily in the areas of tax rates, data privacy and/or security, and records retention.

3. *Client Related Changes.*

    a. The business environment of our clients evolves constantly over time. As their computing needs change, we must modify their systems to meet the new needs.

    b. Every year there are personnel changes in our client base. When a new individual takes on the responsibilities of his or her predecessor, the successor will frequently want to have things done a different way. This may require system changes.

    c. Even with no change in business environment or personnel, clients may find different approaches to their business and request changes to their systems.

From *Software Maintenance: The Problem and Its Solutions,* published in 1983, by James Martin and Carma McClure: "The act of providing what an end user says he needs changes his perception of those needs. The solution to a problem changes the problem."

We have all seen this happen . . . *and it is frustrating!*

4. *Technology.* In no other business has technology required more adaptation more rapidly than in computing. In recent years we have seen incredible changes in the following areas.

    a. End-user computing (EUC) is an established fact. There are very many end users, many of whom no longer need our services.

    b. Microcomputer use has skyrocketed, from use for process control applications a few years ago, to the proliferation of thousands of personal computers for business functions today. Again, some of these people no longer need our services.

    c. Distributed processing has helped the growth of EUC and personal computers. Accountants, analysts, data entry clerks, and others can perform necessary business functions via EUC or on a PC, then easily get the data into other areas, such as central accounting systems.

    d. Communications improvements have also aided the spread of computing. There are now thousands of employees who have the capability of reading and creating data from their homes.

The key to success is understanding these pressures, adapting to them, and developing an approach that allows the business to function in an orderly manner in spite of them.

1.3 SOFTWARE MAINTENANCE—OUR LATEST ENTRY

Maybe there is some truth to the negative picture of maintenance groups painted by the literature. Certainly there was a point in time when our maintenance groups had taken on some of this flavor. To counter that problem, at first we eliminated separate maintenance groups, and spread it around so that everyone had to put up with a little of it.

It soon became apparent, however, that this approach wasn't working either. If our new development was not on schedule, maintenance was always the excuse for its being late. Perhaps a more enlightened approach to separating development and maintenance was in order. We moved with some fear and trepidation (after all, hadn't we just finished the separated approach?) to seek that enlightenment.

The bottom line of this book is that *it did work*. We got the development tasks back on schedule, raised the image of maintenance, and the morale of the maintainers. It is interesting to note that much of what used to be behind-schedule development work is now scheduled maintenance work. And major new development has continued to dwindle, further increasing maintenance as a percentage of the whole.

The first "enlightened" move was to call the separate maintenance group *continuing support*. We wanted to avoid that nasty old word *maintenance*. The group included older people who knew the older systems and their clients well, and didn't want to bother learning new technology. They looked at this assignment positively. They felt they were being allowed to do what they knew how to do. It also included some of the newest members of the staff, who got most of their initial training from the older people, on the older systems.

As the newer people became knowledgeable about the department and the systems to which they were assigned, they were moved on to support some of the new technology systems that had just been developed. Management expended considerable effort letting the entire department know that continuing support was just as important as new development. The aura of classes of citizenship was beginning to disappear.

All members of the group were assigned as primary contact to support one or more systems, and as secondary support for other systems which they were expected to learn. They very quickly were given responsibility for primary client contact. They had to repair jobs that failed, and they had to negotiate modifications and enhancements with their clients. We began capturing data on numbers of repairs and enhancements.

In this way we met one of our objectives, which was to meet target dates on new development. *But we also met the other objective: to create a continuing support group devoid of an image problem.* Since we no longer had major development projects, the entire department worked in this manner. The aura of classes of citizenship was completely gone, since there was only one class of citizen left.

This enlightened approach has needed a periodic shot in the arm, we have learned. Motivational problems seem to be a perennial part of maintenance activity (probably not uniquely). We had to supplement enlightenment with such activities as a work-effectiveness program, which increased participation and improved morale. As part of this effort, we had Daniel Couger (a noted computer scientist and one of the authors of *Maintenance Programming: Improved Productivity Through Motivation*) present a two-day seminar to our managers and managers from other areas of the data processing staff. His advice on treatment of people in maintenance was very insightful.

Before going further into a discussion of what we did, why we did it, and what came of it all, let us pause and lay a foundation for this discussion. In the next section we formulate definitions and examine the literature to lay that foundation.

2

Definitions and the Literature

2.1 SOFTWARE MAINTENANCE—A BRIEF DISCUSSION OF THE LITERATURE

Maintenance programming has been a serious concern in data processing for years. As far back as 1978, GUIDE publication GPP-29, "Productivity in the Maintenance Environment," stated the following in reference to maintenance. *"Measurement and motivation* are considered essential ingredients to determine and enhance the productivity of systems and programming personnel."

How did they even know how productive or unproductive this function was at that time? But the data they gathered indicated that between 65 percent and 80 percent of information systems human resources were being consumed in maintenance. They felt strongly enough about the magnitude of the situation that they concluded, "Maintenance function is no place for new hires, trainees or misfits."

In the intervening years, there have been a number of books, articles, and studies on the subject of maintenance. For the most part, these have been aimed at defining maintenance and suggesting ways to improve the image and productivity of that function.

They have generally painted a picture of ragged, mistreated, undernourished maintenance programmers locked in dungeons with little light or air, and chained to desks cranking out corrections to other people's mistakes. The people who were locked in were the old, the uneducable, the unsalvageable. The bright creative people, usually young, were assigned to work on the outside on new development projects using the latest technology. Those on the outside had visibility, the opportunity to grow, and Muzak. Those on the inside got what they deserved.

Girish Parikh in a *Computerworld* article titled "Software maintenance: penny wise, program foolish," September 23, 1985, says, "Programmers change jobs every 1.5 years on the average. . . . Ironically, the frustrating maintenance work itself contributes to the high programmer turnover. . . . Perhaps the reason lies in programmers' general dislike for software maintenance. Some even hate the work." Certainly, our early experiences support these comments.

One of the better known books on the subject of maintenance was written by William E. Perry in 1983, *Managing Systems Maintenance.* This book helped us focus our efforts on identifying and gathering metrics.

For the purpose of his book, Mr. Perry defined maintenance as "all of the activities involved in keeping application systems working in a condition satisfactory to all involved parties." Our department operated on essentially this definition. He says there are three types of maintenance.

1. errors
2. new requirements
3. enhancements

In *Software Maintenance: The Problem and Its Solutions,* James Martin and Carma McClure point out that even though maintenance consumes a very large share of the software dollar, it has been almost totally ignored in the literature. (A major reason for having written this book.) They state that the term *maintenance* refers to "changes that have to be made to computer programs after they have been delivered to the customer or user." They proceed to say that it includes corrections, design enhancements, and adjustments to program behavior, and that corrections consume only 20 percent of the maintenance work. In our shop that figure is only about 5 percent to 6 percent.

Some authors contend that enhancements in program function are an inappropriate subfunction of maintenance, but that this is now firmly embedded in current terminology. I disagree with this point. If I wanted an upgrade applied to my car, I would take it to a repair (maintenance) shop, not back to the factory.

Mr. Martin and Ms. McClure point out one of the less obvious costs of maintenance is eventual rigidity. They state that over time, a system can become so fragile that the DP department is reluctant to tamper with it. After a while, this can become almost invisible.

Several years ago, I was discussing with a member of my management those systems which I thought should be replaced or significantly rewritten. Of course, the annual maintenance cost of each of the systems was an important part of the conversation. One of those I mentioned had a relatively low annual maintenance cost, so he asked me if the client wanted a lot of enhancements. I told him they had not asked for an enhancement for over a year because they were tired of being turned down. For the last several years we had become more reluctant with each enhancement we installed.

Finally, the clients got so tired of hearing our reasons for not installing the next enhancement that they quit asking.

This is a major system I am referring to. I don't know how much more function the clients really need or want, or what additional function would be worth to the company, but until the system is replaced, little or nothing about it will be changed. Our concerns about making changes to this system are clearly defensible.

Various studies have indicated that on the average, changing an existing program is three times as error-prone as writing new code. This particular system is one of the oldest and most complex in our shop, and changes would surely be more error-prone than the average. Martin and McClure also refer to chain reactions, to which this system would surely be subjected by any modifications.

In 1985 J. Daniel Couger and Mel A. Colter published a book entitled *Maintenance Programming: Improved Productivity Through Motivation.* The book reports a maintenance study they conducted in ten major companies. This study clearly portrays the dungeon image of maintenance. It is a continuation of the work Couger and Robert Zawacki had written about in their book *Motivating and Managing Computer Personnel,* which is largely based on matching the "Growth Need Strength (GNS)" of programmers and others with the "Motivating Potential Score (MPS)" of their jobs.

Couger and Colter identified two components of maintenance: (1) fixit; and (2) enhancement. They went on to say that they have not defined any clear line of demarcation between enhancement and new development. In dealing with what they refer to as traditional maintenance, they conclude *"the higher the percentage of maintenance, the lower the motivating potential of the job"* (italics added). Their recommendation is to redesign the maintenance jobs, using as a framework, the following five core job dimensions:

1. Skill variety: degree to which the job requires use of different skills
2. Task identity: degree to which the job requires completion of a "whole" identifiable piece of work
3. Task significance: degree to which job has a substantial impact on the lives or work of other people
4. Autonomy: degree to which the job provides substantial freedom, independence, and discretion to the employee
5. Feedback from the job itself: degree to which carrying out the work activities results in employee obtaining information about the effectiveness of his or her performance

The authors relate a number of cases where this was done and state that productivity in those cases improved. In one particular case, "the company was able to enhance its motivational environment significantly—resulting in increased productivity." Elsewhere they state, "The view of non-productivity of the programmers was based on their inability to meet schedules for completing change requests and to reduce the large backlog of change requests."

This is approximately what we did in our early efforts, and exactly what we did later on with work effectiveness programs, and it works!

In the GUIDE publication GPP-130, "Maintenance Productivity Improvements Through Matrices and Measurements," copyrighted in 1985, maintenance is defined as "correction of errors and the enhancement of the business process."

The publication identifies the six following categories, and the percentage of time spent on each by survey respondents.

Category	Percent of time
1. Repair	8
2. Enhancement	54
3. Conversion	2
4. User support	11
5. Prevention	3
6. Nonproject	22

Abbreviated definitions follow.

1. Repair: correct defects created by maintenance group
2. Enhancement: add function to the system
3. Conversion: hardware/software modification with no change in function
4. User support: consulting, correct defects created by others
5. Prevention: avert foreseeable problems or save money
6. Nonproject: related overhead including vacation, administrative work, training, and so on

It was concluded that to measure maintenance, an organization must have categories to measure, and systems for problem reporting, request tracking, and labor tracking. Also suggested are some specific metrics, which are included later in this book.

And finally, in an article in *Computerworld,* April 8, 1985, "Maintenance push is on," T. Capers Jones III says that *"maintenance . . . is gradually being recognized as a major technical discipline with its own unique productivity and quality characteristics."* He also reports on an experiment with 26 maintenance programmers which indicated that changes could be made to a well-structured and cleanly segmented program in about one fourth the time it would take for a poorly structured program.

We agreed with these points. Over a two year period, we developed a categorization scheme and have tracked time spent in each. More details are reported in Chapter 3.3.

Summary

Looking at the statements of all of the authorities referenced here, one can only conclude that maintenance, like truth and beauty, is in the eye of the beholder. There is no commonly accepted definition of the function, or the activities included therein. But a couple of good points can be gleaned from these authorities.

1. People who are treated well will perform better than people who are treated poorly. Treating software maintainers with dignity and respect yields better results than treating them as second-class citizens.
2. Categorize the work done in the maintenance area, whatever you perceive the categories to be. The application of metrics to the work that is done will eventually provide more insight about that work, and about what can be done to improve the performance of that work.

2.2 PERFORMANCE—WHAT WE'RE TRYING TO ACHIEVE _____

Most business people will agree that the primary objective of any staff department is to improve their performance in order to have the desired positive effect on profit. But to improve performance, we must first understand what it is, and deal with its individual components: *productivity, quality, and professionalism.* The actual relationship is:

$$\text{Performance} = (\text{Quality} \times \text{Quantity}) + \text{Professionalism}$$

In this equation, quantity is used to represent a specific level of productivity. The equation is not intended to imply that a numerical value can always be applied to performance. However, the clear implication is that if either quality or quantity is zero, then performance is nothing more than professionalism.

Furthermore, professionalism, which can be negative as well as positive, can have a powerful effect on the level of performance (and of course on the career of the individual). Professionalism is used here to account for an individual's degree of pride in his or her work, energy level, and attitude toward the work as well as toward other employees. Thus, to impact performance, we must affect quality, productivity, and/or professionalism.

The performance range of most people is fixed by the time they go to work for you. However, their actual performance level will vary considerably in this range depending on external factors, primarily your management of them.

The three components of quality, productivity, and professionalism can all be affected by motivation and capability. Thus, looked at from another perspective

$$\text{Performance} = \text{Motivation} \times \text{Capability}$$

Again, note the multiplicative function. If one is zero, the result is zero.

Thus, to improve performance, we must work with the components of motivation and capability. Capability is discussed in Chapter 2.5. Motivation is the subject of Chapter 3.1.

And from one final perspective, effectiveness and efficiency are aspects of productivity. Effectiveness is doing the right things. And efficiency is doing things right.

2.3 METRICS

People seem to have an unquenchable thirst to measure everything they can. We measure our own size, our weight, the clothes we wear (what are the units of size 10?), our cars (MPG, speed, wheelbase), our houses (rooms, square feet), the pressure and temperature of the air we breathe, the amount of light we read by, the level of sound we hear, the size of our planet and our universe, the value of our assets, and much more. About the only thing we don't seem to have an interest in measuring is the limit on what we want to measure. Furthermore, it is apparent that the better we can measure things (within reason), the better we can do them. It's no wonder we have been expending considerable effort in trying to measure information systems. We seem to feel that something is missing without such measurements. Maybe we are even a little embarrassed that other business functions can measure what they do and we can't.

Although everything about measuring seems positive, there is at least one drawback. We sometimes feel so **confident** about what we can measure and so **inadequate** about what we cannot measure that we emphasize the former to the exclusion of the latter. For example, we are frequently very uneasy about a capital investment, on which the return is intangible, even though we are certain that the investment is a good one. If we could measure the benefits on the bottom line, there would be no hesitation—because this is what we were taught to understand. Maybe this is why St. Louis County announced that plans were in progress to build a 70,000-seat, multimillion-dollar stadium complex just one week after a school bond issue failed in St. Louis City.

The danger here is that measurement might become the end rather than the means. We must be able to keep open minds so we won't miss the *"aha's"* we will turn up with our measurements. When we put all of the numbers together and something looks wrong, we ask why. It is the answers to the "why's" that produce the "aha's." We must keep constant watch for these "aha's." They are the signposts that provide our direction, our bread and butter. Yours will be different from mine, but we all need to identify those metrics which will be relevant in our individual shops.

Measurements in a data processing shop can be looked upon as instrumentation or productivity measures in a plant. Measurement at a point in time can be meaningful if the metric is familiar. If you get up in the morning, and hear on the radio that the current temperature is 72 degrees, this is meaningful. You know how to dress because of your familiarity with this metric.

Since there is very little available today in the area of effective, accepted programmer metrics, it is apparent that we must establish new metrics for this environment. Because they will be new, they will be useful only over a period of time, during which we can become familiar with them, determine trends, modify them, combine them, and verify their reasonableness and usefulness. We will encounter problems in the identification, definition, and application of our new metrics. These may be better solved by use of ingenuity than by expertise.

For example, if we determine that on the average a programmer is responsible for maintenance of 92 programs, or on the average, a production program fails every 7,528 processings, we have very little familiarity with these metrics; therefore, do not know the full meaning of them. New metrics have no history or similar circumstances to which they can be related. *Without relationships, metrics are not very useful.*

But over time, <u>metrics need not be perfect to be useful.</u> Order of magnitude and/or trend will normally accomplish the purposes of measuring. In metrics, just as in most fields, *imperfect does not mean invalid.*

Watch out for balancing. Accountants live for things to balance. To them, $1 out of balance on a $10,000,000 payables file spells big trouble. Not so in the wonderful world of software metrics. If you set up a metrics program, you will be gathering much data from many different sources, and there will be many gray areas in these categories. It will be common to be out of balance. Further, you will sometimes be using data which you know contain a percentage of error. *Remember, precision is not the key to improvement. Trend is a key. Why one number looks out of place is another key.*

For example, our abend rate went from 5.3 percent in one year to 3.9 percent the next. *That is a 26% improvement.* Is it important that the improvement might have been 15 percent or 35 percent? We state that our productivity increased by 38 percent per year for a four-year period, based on modules maintained per person. This is a big improvement. The point is that management understands that we made a big improvement. It is not terribly important to them whether it was ¼, or ⅓, or ½. We can work on precision after we have identified direction.

Even though we know ahead of time that it will be very difficult, we must try to identify and capture what metrics we can. In *Programming Productivity*, Capers Jones states: "Before any technology can be evaluated, it must be measurable." He then goes on to point out the *depressing* fact that "Programming has proven to be one of the most difficult human activities to measure or quantify."[1]

In 1981, GUIDE International published GPP-65, "Measurement of Productivity." The publication includes the following statements. *"Attention given by management to monitoring performance often can provide the impetus for the staff to improve the index which is being tracked. This alone may provide sufficient cause for measuring productivity."* Among their conclusions are:

1. Measurement should be used to determine trend over an extended period of time.
2. It can identify areas where more effort is needed.
3. It provides answers to upper management.
4. It is useful for cost/benefit studies.
5. It is useful in forecasting.

An article titled "A Structured Approach to MIS Productivity Measurement" published in the *Journal of Information Systems Management* in the fall of 1985 reports on an effort undertaken in the IS department of an oil field equipment firm. They state that one of their problems was "the premature concern for how to measure productivity rather than what was the appropriate characteristic to measure."

---

[1]Capers Jones, *Programming Productivity*, McGraw-Hill, 1986. Reprinted with permission

They split the measurement of productivity into the measurements of effectiveness and efficiency. Their measurements of effectiveness are of the "softer," qualitative type, such as fitness for use and user friendliness.

Their measurements of efficiency are quantitative, and are based on outputs produced by IS and delivered to the client. The items they identified follow.

1. IMS transactions
2. TSO transactions
3. Printed lines of reports
4. Number of microfiche cards
5. Storage space on disk and tape

They refer to the preceding items as "standard products" and they identify yearly output as the total of these delivered to their clients. Though I don't buy this completely, this is as good an identification of the output of an IS department as I have seen yet.

In *Software Productivity*, Harlan Mills writes the following about work which he started more than twenty years ago.

> "My search for productivity in software has uncovered no magic, no panaceas. There are remarkable improvements possible over today's accepted levels. But they require sound methodology and sound management. Mastering the methodology requires an intellectual commitment of several years. If it were easier, everybody would be doing it already."

That's the bad news. But he follows this up shortly with the good news.

> "Computer programming is less than a generation old. . . . it took many generations of brilliant minds to evolve geometry into a well organized subject."

and

> "500 years ago, no one knew that air had weight. . . Complexity has a "weight" of some kind, but we do not know what it is."

The future lies ahead!

Why Should We Measure Our Work?

Management requires information to do its job of planning, controlling, organizing, directing, and decision making. Measurement helps identify strengths and weaknesses so that appropriate action can be taken to emphasize the strengths or correct the weaknesses. The following reasons are more specific.

1. Predictability:
   - We need the ability to predict/estimate for the future.
   - We need this each year in budgeting.
   - We need it for cost and time estimating for projects.
   - We need the ability to plan.

2. Quality:
   - We need to know how well we meet the needs of our clients individually and as a group.
   - We need to know how effective our products are.
   - We need to know if we are doing better, worse, or the same so that we can evaluate our efforts at improvement.

3. Productivity:
   - We need to know if our products are justifiable.
   - We need to know how efficient our products are individually and as a group.
   - We need to know how efficient is our use of data processing resources.
   - We need to know if we are doing better, worse, or the same in order to evaluate our efforts at improvement.

4. Control:
   - We need to track the results of our efforts so that we may make necessary adjustments.

5. Motivation:
   - It has been demonstrated that *awareness will modify behavior*. People will try to achieve the goals set, if they are reasonable. (The "Schwab Effect." See chapter on motivation.)

6. Upward Communications:
   - To answer the questions of upper-level management before they are asked.

It should be noted that there is a big difference in the value of measuring in a maintenance environment versus an operating environment. Generally, operating decisions can be verified as to correctness by observing the production line shortly after the decision is made. In a maintenance environment, it may take several years to determine the effect of a decision.

According to William E. Perry, "What you cannot measure, you cannot control."

On the other hand, George Odiorne, author and lecturer, has said in *Management Decisions by Objectives*, "Measure the measurable. If it can't be measured, describe the describable. *If it's undescribable, stop doing it.*" We have at least described what we expect.

What Should We Measure?

It is suggested that we start by measuring just about anything we can inexpensively obtain, rather than try to identify every meaningful metric at the beginning. Keep in mind that people are like electrons. They will follow the path of least resistance. If the metrics selected require significant extra effort to obtain, the people will try to go around them.

The boss can stand in the path of least resistance with a baseball bat so that the people will use the desired path. This, however, may create a serious morale problem. And eventually, when the boss gets bored with this, the people will return to their favored path. *We must strive to make the path of metrics the path of least resistance.*

Further, we must select metrics which are perceived as tamper resistant, reliable, and valid. The best metrics are those which can be obtained by automated means. This is cheaper than manual methods, and is not as threatening to the person whose work is being measured, nor to the person doing the measuring. If there is a degree of uncertainty of the value of the metric, but it is not difficult to capture, get it. It can always be dropped later. But you cannot go back in time to get it if you find at a later date that it would have been beneficial.

Several times I was asked to provide historical data about a particular activity. Occasionally, I was able to retrieve the data from my "electronic trash can" with little effort, as these were items I had been capturing for some time.

Lowell Jay Arthur in his book *Measuring Programmer Productivity and Software Quality* makes two points I would like to emphasize here. First, he says "The most critical factors affecting productivity, such as employee morale and client concern, will be the most difficult to measure." Also, "any attempt to measure software productivity and quality without mechanization will require a large amount of manual effort at a prohibitive cost."

Following is a list of statistics that can be used to measure change. It is compiled from a number of different sources. You will see later in the book the context in which we used some of the items to get our points across to our management. Three different types of "employee counts" are used for different measures: programmer/analysts, professionals, and employees. Professionals are the programmer/analysts and their managers, and the addition of secretaries gives total employees in the department. Review the list and consider what you might be able to capture readily in your shop.

1. Number of programs moved to production per month per programmer/analyst (P/A)
2. Number of compiles/program moved
3. Abends/production run (failures/processing)
4. Maintenance cost/year per program in production
5. Staff utilization = time billed divided by total time available
6. Average revenue generated per employee
7. Millions of dollars of inventory/professional
8. Production moves/year/module maintained
9. Compiles/year/module maintained
10. Percent employee turnover
11. Client satisfaction (survey each year)—record complaints and compliments as they happen

12. Number of production changes/programmer/month
13. Failures/production change
14. Failures/month/production program
15. Failures/month/programmer
16. Mean time between job failures
17. Programs supported/programmer
18. Number of night calls per program in production
19. Maintenance cost/year per 1,000 lines of code in production
20. Maintenance cost/year of a system over development cost of that system
21. Estimates versus actuals
22. Number of projects or work requests completed per year by category. This, of course, implies the need to define those categories.
23. Percent of group time spent in each category
24. Work requests received per day per group
25. Work requests completed per day per group
26. Number of work requests per system per year
27. PATHVU (a tool discussed in Chapter 3.2) level of production programs
28. Millions of dollars of production/professional
29. Number of contractors/number of professionals
30. Cost/significant activity in a system, such as:
    a. Cost/check written in Salary Payroll and Payables
    b. Cost/order taken in Order Billing
    c. Cost/requisition in Procurement
    d. Cost/update transaction in other systems such as Property
31. Value of assets maintained per system, such as:
    a. Value of checks written by Salary Payroll
    b. Value of orders taken by Order Billing
    c. Value of requisitions generated by Procurement
    d. Value of assets maintained in Property System
32. Machine dollars/people dollar

How To Gather Some Of The Suggested Measurements

1. *Number of programs moved to production per month per P/A.* Each month we captured headcount by job title from our personnel group. We had a procedure which was required to move a program to production status. The programs moved are captured in a data set which includes the name of the analyst who moved the program, and the name of the project manager of the analyst. It is then a simple matter to perform the division. Trends and points of high activity can be identified from this measurement.

2. *Number of compiles/program moved to production.* The number of compiles is extracted from SMF records generated by IBM mainframes. The SMF records are read, and those which indicate the compiler was executed are written on another file for analysis. This statistic gives a general idea of the thoroughness of the programming staff.

IBM mainframe computers generate System Management Facilities (SMF) records which include large quantities of data about system tasks, including batch jobs. These records may be used to generate various statistics about what is being processed on the computer. Among other things, CPU time and I/O activity are recorded. Also, system completion codes are included, which can be used to determine reliability of certain jobs or groups of jobs.

3. *Abends/production run (failures/processing—batch).* Again, the SMF records are read. It is a simple matter of counting jobs with a zero abend code and those with a nonzero code. The nonzeros are captured on another file for further analysis. This has been used to track trends in abend rate and identified its seasonality.

4. *Maintenance cost/year per program in production.* All of our production programs were maintained on LIBRARIAN files specified for this purpose. The annual budget was divided by this number of programs. This gave an indication of productivity trend.

LIBRARIAN is a program library. We used it primarily for source code and test data, but it can be used for object code and general data. Program lines are identified by line number, and version numbers are tracked by the system. By using different LIBRARIAN data set names for each of our groups, we were able to easily track lines of code and number of modules by departmental group. When we used it, it was a product of Applied Data Research (ADR), but is now marketed by Computer Associates International, Inc., 711 Stewart Ave., Garden City, NY 11530, 1-800-645-3003.

5. *Staff utilization = time billed/total time available.* We recorded all time in PAC II. Each project had an account associated with it. And all of the accounts were identified as billable or nonbillable. With this basic data it is easy to identify this ratio. We tried to keep it above 80 percent. When it went below, we could usually identify the reason.

PAC II is a "Project Accounting and Control" system. It was used at Monsanto for many years for project planning, assigning programmers and analysts, after-the-fact project record keeping, and time recording for billing purposes. The vendor of the product is A.G.S, King of Prussia, PA, a subsidiary of Nynex.

6. *Average revenue generated per employee.* The accounting system yields revenue. The ratio is simple. This also gives an indication of productivity trend.

7. *Millions of dollars of inventory/professional.* Number of lines of code was available weekly in the production LIBRARIAN. We were using $25 per line as the inventory cost. The ratio is simple. Again, this is an indicator of productivity trend.

8. *Production moves/year/module maintained.* Source for production moves is stated in number 1 earlier. Source for modules is the same LIBRARIAN as stated in number 4 earlier. This is a simple ratio which gives an indication of the turnover rate of our inventory.

9. *Compiles/year/module maintained.* Source for compiles is stated in number 2 earlier. Source for modules is the same LIBRARIAN as stated previously in number 4. This ratio gives an indication of the amount of effort which goes into supporting the production code.

RAW DATA NEEDED (MONTHLY)

1. Headcount by job type
2. Programs in production
3. Modules in production
4. Programs moved to production
5. Other production changes
6. Production abends
7. Compiles
8. Number of production processings
9. Budget amounts
10. Where people-hours are charged
11. Number of lines of code (to get inventory value)

2.4 QUALITY—WHAT IS IT?

Quality is a particularly sticky point. According to the dictionary, *quality* is defined as "degree of excellence." *Degree* is "relative intensity or amount." And *relative* is "dependent upon or interconnected with something else for intelligibility or significance." This circles back to my original understanding that *quality is how good something is as compared to something else.* So I still have no finite, commonly agreeable definition of quality against which things can be numerically measured. *If employees have no definition of quality, and no numerical target to strive for, it is difficult for them to be motivated to achieve it.*

For these reasons, quality has been redefined by several authorities, so that it might be specified, measured, and achieved. The definition stated by J. M. Juran is:

Quality Means Fitness for Use.

The word *use* in this definition includes the following items beyond the primary intended use of the product.

- low waste levels

- low repair levels
- good documentation
- good packaging
- stability
- low rate of complaints
- et cetera

The quality mission for a company is usually fitness for use. The quality mission for a department or individual is usually conformance to specifications. Juran uses the example of the drug Thalidomide. It was probably produced by departments and individuals in compliance to specifications. However, the company failed the quality test in that the product was not fit for use.

Key ingredients in the quest for quality are the need for employees to know what is expected, and to have the tools available to achieve those expectations. Before people can be held responsible for quality work, they must be provided with an environment in which quality can be achieved. They must:

1. know what they should be doing
2. know what they are doing
3. have the skills, tools, and authority to comply

When specifying standards, however, don't set them unnecessarily high. Set them at the level appropriate to the situation. Everyone agrees that quality—like motherhood, apple pie, and the flag—is good, but quality in excess of what is needed and/or desired by the clients or potential clients is not beneficial. Keep in mind that internal "perfectionism" adds costs to you, but not your competitors. But also be sure that you and the clients have the same understanding of the level of quality to be provided.

There are two reasons to provide different degrees of quality. The first is the expectations of the client based on the cost and requirements. If you bought a $3,000 used car and the window crank came off in your hand, you might just press it back in place and figure that's life. If the same kind of thing happened in your new Rolls Royce, you would probably be extremely upset, as your expectations would have been severely disappointed.

If the client requests a quick, simple, inexpensive program to forecast next year's consumption of office supplies, he or she does not expect to pay a significant sum for quality assurance and testing. On the other hand, if the client needs a central cost system as the basis of controlling the business, and reporting to stockholders and regulatory agencies, the need is obviously for a much higher degree of quality than the previous case. The client would expect to pay for the quality, reliability, and accuracy required, and would demand to receive it.

The second reason has to do with the criticality of the situation. Medical devices which provide life or death information to physicians require extremely high quality.

And military devices such as missile guidance systems require the ultimate in quality. No one wants to buy a missile that might land in their own back yard . . . or for that matter, in any unintended location. And in these cases, the client will *expect* to pay a large amount for quality assurance and testing.

Another authority on the subject of quality is William E. Perry, Executive Director of the Quality Assurance Institute. According to Mr. Perry,

"Quality Is Compliance to a Standard."

It is an integral part of any science and/or process, and you can't have it without a process. You can't have it in an art form. It is part attitude. It is everybody's job.

He goes on to say if you can define quality, you can measure it. If you can measure it, you can control it. Without measurement standards, programmers are playing golf in a fog. They need measurable feedback. To be successful, they must know from moment to moment where they stand (feedback from the job). Quality assurance cannot work if data processing is viewed as an art, but only if it is viewed as a science. Quality control can be a major motivator.

Further, Mr. Perry says quality and productivity must be measured as variances from established standards, and that setting such standards can cause behavior to change. Individuals will generally attempt to achieve stated goals. If, for example, we pay for more lines of code, we will get more lines of code, probably to the detriment of quality. (See the "Schwab Effect" in the chapter on motivation.)

The motto of quality assurance (QA) is "Do it right the first time."

Along this same line of reasoning, in *Quality Is Free* Phillip B. Crosby wrote, "Error is not required to fulfill the laws of nature." He makes an interesting point of people's attitudes about quality. He says that we have a double standard in that we accept defects at work which we would not accept in our personal lives. We would not accept nurses occasionally dropping babies, being shortchanged, or paying for an unacceptable product.

According to Claude Burrill and Leon Ellsworth, quality is not an added cost because "*it is always cheaper to do the job right the first time rather than to do it over.*" Furthermore, they state that quality cannot be achieved unless it can be measured, and it cannot be measured unless it can first be defined. Their definition of quality follows:

"Quality Means Meeting Requirements."

Part of their proof of this definition is a comparison of a Cadillac and a Chevrolet, stating that if both meet their particular requirements, then both are quality products.

Why then are so many Japanese cars sold in the United States? Is it because the Japanese provide more function, comfort, or convenience at a lower price? No. It is because of the perceived superior quality of these Japanese products by American car buyers.

The typical buyer of automobiles does not state specific maintenance/ dependability requirements. But Americans buy a lot of Japanese cars because they have had better maintenance records (are more dependable) than American cars in recent years. We apparently have aversions to repair shop waiting rooms, or walking home from our vehicles.

Thus, car buyers perceive that Japanese cars are of higher quality. The nonspecific requirement upon which this perception is based is lower maintenance—or better dependability. So while all of the cars "meet the specifications," there is still a perceptual difference in degree of quality on the part of car buyers. Data processing has to deal with those same perceptual differences on the part of our clients.

Burrill and Ellsworth further state that part of any product requirement list must include the quality requirements. They too make the point that employees cannot be held responsible for quality if there are no stated quality requirements. But later on they say that

> many quality requirements cannot be quantified, at least not with our present understanding. Standards for the design of a data system, much like standards for a novel, are stated largely in qualitative terms. Compliance cannot be confirmed simply by counting or measuring; it requires judgement by a trained professional.

There has been considerable discussion in the literature for years about the source of quality problems. One source that always seems to float to the top is requirements definition. *How can we measure quality based on the definition of meeting requirements when we have admitted that our ability to define requirements is one of our biggest shortcomings?* Lowell Jay Arthur makes an excellent related point in *Programmer Productivity: Myths, Methods, and Murphology,* published in 1983. He states, "If the system doesn't meet the user's needs (not necessarily the requirements), it is of poor quality."

And in *The Psychology of Computer Programming* published in 1971, Gerald M. Weinberg has a chapter on what makes a "good program." (This was in the days before quality was a major topic of discussion.) In it he said, "any program that works is better than any program that doesn't." He goes on to say that "there are degrees of meeting specifications," and "The question of what makes a good program is not a simple one, and may not even be a proper question."

On the one hand, most of the authorities previously cited agree that quality can be defined as meeting requirements, or fit for use, or something similar. But then they soften this sharp definition by at least implying that *quality is extremely difficult to define, is qualitative, is judgmental, and includes such concepts as better, worse, higher, and lower.*

After some discussion in our department, we agreed that the data processing community had already invented and redefined too many words. We agreed that the definition of quality in the dictionary was a good one, and one that we could live with—*but could not measure against.* And we also agreed that meeting requirements is a part of quality, but only one part.

So let's not create a new definition. Let's describe the components we hope to use for measurement because just telling a programmer to meet specifications is not enough. Many of the publications cited previously include what they call facets or characteristics of quality. Following are those components which we chose to emphasize in our department.

Components of Quality

Meeting the specifications is one component of quality which is readily quantifiable. We call it *functionality*. It either does what it is supposed to do, or it does not.

The only other component of quality that is quantifiable is *reliability*. This is the percent of time that a product does what it is supposed to do. It is essentially the inverse of the abend ratio, or failure rate.

All of the remaining components are *degree* or *relationship* types of measurements. They are subjective and require a relationship to another similar product, or to the same product at a different point in time. But let's not ignore them just because they require "professional judgment" to measure.

Integrity is the degree to which a system can handle garbage in, filter it, and still produce good results.

Efficiency is the reasonableness of the cost to process the product compared with other products, or another time period.

Maintainability is the speed and/or ease with which modifications can be made, either due to bugs or requested changes.

Ease of use, or user friendliness, is the quickness to learn and the simplicity to use.

Flexibility is the number of different ways to get things done with the product. Can you take a shortcut once you know your way around? Or must you always follow the same long path?

Uniqueness is the amount of creativity, ingenuity, and/or original thought that was required to create the product. Keep in mind that 98 percent of the wheels have already been invented, and in most cases uniqueness is not desired. However, in those 2 percent of the cases where a new wheel is called for, this is the place to make note of it.

And of course, *client satisfaction* is of overriding importance. All of the preceding components influence this one. We tried to measure this with an annual questionnaire.

Cost of Quality

Harold Geneen said, "Quality is not only right, it is free. And it is not only free, it is the most profitable product line we have." *The truth of the matter is that it is not free, but it is very profitable.* Furthermore, something is being spent on quality—even if you think it's not. Quality costs always show up in one or more of the following areas.

1. *Prevention*—doing the job right the first time. These costs are incurred before the product is built, and include methods, procedures, training, and planning.
2. *Appraisal*—comparing the product with requirements, at milestones, and at the end. It includes inspections, testing, and reviews.
3. Failure—defective products. This includes doing work over, delays in getting a return on investment, lost time of clients, or even lost clients, and so forth. Failure is always the largest component of the cost of quality.

To avoid the cost of failure, resources must be expended on prevention and/or appraisal. Thus, *quality is never free, but it is most often an excellent investment.*

Summary

Quality, and probably productivity in our business as well, are a lot like the Loch Ness Monster. Everybody has heard of it. And some people claim to have seen it. But nobody can yet say that they have captured it.

Quality is all but impossible to adequately define, but people feel the need for specifics against which to measure achievement. Similarly, people don't like the subjectivity of performance appraisals, but having admitted that they are subjective, we continue to do performance appraisals—judgment and all.

So let's not hide behind new definitions of old words. Let's admit that there are degrees of quality which require judgment to identify. And just publish the components and a description of the cost of quality, tell the employees what is expected with all of the metrics we have available, and the expected will be achieved. This is the approach we took, and it was a significant part of our success.

Quality has always been a difficult thing to measure. And so has software. Both are intangible—there is nothing there to reach out and grasp, to hold in your hand, to weigh or to size.

So it is not surprising that we in software have had problems throughout the history of our discipline measuring the quality of the products we produce. What is surprising, however, is that we have missed some valid analogies in other fields that could help us with this dilemma.

Is there another field with an intangible product and a deep need to measure quality? One author (unfortunately, the source of this suggestion, is mired irretrievably in the musty recesses of the second author's memory) has suggested that there is. The essence of athletic competition in the Olympics is in the measured quality of a performance. For some sports, such as those involving times and distances, it is easy to select winners based on quality of performance. For others, such as gymnastics and diving, quality is a judgment call. So how do athletic competitions score quality when it's intangible? They select a panel of expert judges to make those judgment calls. And they average the scores of the judges.

Quality measurement, literally, becomes a judgment call. Could this same idea be used to evaluate software quality?

2.5 PRODUCTIVITY AND CAPABILITY _____

Again, I went to the dictionary—this time for the definition of productivity. The dictionary says that productivity is output divided by input. This leaves only half a problem, as we can readily measure input in hours, days, and dollars. *Unfortunately, we cannot yet define or measure our output.*

To Robert Blake and Jane Mouton in *Productivity: The Human Side,* "Nothing in the industrial setting is more important than improving productivity." They give the following three reasons for making this statement.

1. It provides a better standard of living.
2. It keeps the nation competitive in world trade.
3. Productive people are happy people.

According to Burrill and Ellsworth, productivity is measured by the value or worth of the products produced—and the value of a product is most frequently identified by the price paid for it. Thus, in an external business arrangement, the productivity would be the ratio of the price (output) to the cost (input). But in many data processing organizations there is no charge-back to the clients. And even when there is charge-back, it is usually at cost. Thus, at best, our productivity level measured on this basis would be "1," and it would not reflect any changes actually made in productivity.

In *Programming Productivity,* Capers Jones states that productivity is a "surprisingly ambiguous" term. In his discussions on software productivity, he has identified two common concerns. The first is elapsed development time, and the second is the cost of software. Later, he cites a study he made for IBM between 1973 and 1978 in which he concluded that projects with rapid schedules as high priority objectives more often exceed schedules and budgets than projects with quality as a high-priority objective. *The implication is that a tight schedule is not consistent with a quality product.*

While doing this research, I came across a PC package called "Productivity Measurement System," which is used to track productivity trends, and is endorsed by the American Bankers Association. I attended a presentation by Nicki Bjornson, President of Impact Systems, Inc., the vendor of the product.

To use the system, one must first identify product outputs, select a base period (say last year), then determine the number of hours required to generate a unit of output during that base period. Subsequently, you merely track the monthly product outputs per hour of input, which provides the productivity trend. Furthermore, since this package was developed for banking, and has been installed in a number of banks, the vendor already has a considerable list of product outputs.

At the end of the presentation, I asked how this might be used in various departments and she had good answers until we got to data processing. She said this has worked well in data entry and operations, but they have "studiously avoided" its use in systems and programming because their product is "process" oriented and that systems and programming are "project" oriented.

I therefore concluded that not even people in the productivity measurement business have learned how to measure software development yet.

Furthermore, it occurs to me that even if we could identify discrete output units today, such as lines of code, number of changes made, function points added or changed, reports and transactions added or changed, this would not answer the productivity question. Before these units can really be meaningful, we must be able to quantify quality.

Imagine two programmers, each responsible for maintaining 100 programs with a total of 100,000 lines of code each. With only this information, can we say that the one who changed six function points is twice as productive as the one who changed three in the same time? Is the one who changed four reports twice as productive as the one who changed two in the same time?

Even if we assume that the changes are all of identical magnitude, the answer is *it depends on the relative quality of the code they are maintaining*. This clearly makes the point that productivity is not merely output units divided by input units, but the output must be made up of units that satisfy the quality requirements. Furthermore, in identifying the productivity of software maintenance, the relative quality of the product being maintained is of critical significance.

Let's consider another analogy here. Two truck drivers are given the identical assignment of moving loads of product from the plant to the warehouse. The job is simple. Load the truck at the plant, drive to the warehouse, unload the truck, drive back to the plant, and start over. At the end of the week Harvey has moved 50 loads while Fred has moved only 25 loads.

Is Harvey twice as productive as Fred? Sure. Is this a meaningful productivity metric? Not yet. We must find out why there is a difference. Suppose that Harvey has a new truck, and Fred's truck can't make it the whole distance without a break-down. Suppose Fred has been spending 60 percent of his time fixing his truck. Maybe Fred is really the more productive employee.

But this is a simple problem. We understand that Fred has a quality problem with his truck (or he's a terrible mechanic). We do a little analysis of the cost of his time, the cost of a new (or better) truck, and the need to move more loads to the warehouse. And on the basis of this analysis, we make an intelligent business decision to buy or not to buy another truck.

It's much more complicated in software metrics because we don't understand software quality very well and have not yet been able to measure it satisfactorily. The business decision, easily made in the truck case, is much more difficult here.

By analogy then, it seems to me that *measuring quality is the first step in meaningful productivity metrics*.

So, until we have a better handle on quality metrics, let's back down, as we did in the case of quality, to the components of productivity. Again, if the employees know what is being observed—if not actually measured—they will achieve it. Hence, the following.

Components of Productivity

The relationships of the components of productivity can be shown as follows.

Productivity is the result of Capability times Motivation.

Capability comes from Skills and Tools.

Skills come from Experience, Education, Training, and Practices.

Practices are made up of Policies, Methods, Standards, and Guidelines.

Motivation is composed of Attitude, Development, Recognition,
and Expectations.

From this perspective, the two primary components of productivity are the capability of the individual and his or her motivation to do the job.

Logically, these two components are multiplicative. If the individual is incapable of doing the assigned task (say, lifting 10,000 pounds barehanded), then no amount of motivation will produce the desired result. If there is no motivation to do a task (dig a small hole in the ground for no reward), then no amount of capability will produce the desired result.

Thus, it can be seen that the level of productivity can be affected from either of two main approaches—motivation and capability. The former is the subject of Chapter 3.1. The latter is discussed in what follows.

What To Do To Improve Productivity

1. Hire people with the innate ability to do the job or to learn to do the job.
2. When a mistake becomes apparent in this area (and there will be some mistakes), rectify it quickly.
3. Train the people to do the job well.
4. Teach them how the job fits into the whole.
5. Provide proper tools for the job, but not so many tools that they become difficult to keep organized.
6. As newer tools become available, replace the older tools. (If the old tools are not discarded, they become clutter.)
7. Provide standards and procedures for doing the job efficiently.
8. Provide a creative atmosphere which encourages internal motivation.
9. Measure the results.
10. Provide large quantities of feedback.

Capability

How do we improve capability? Again, let's break it down. As previously stated, the primary components are skills and tools. The tools are part of the environment we provide with respect to hardware and software. We can increase an individual's capability by simply investing in better tools. We have been doing this in our business since the beginning, and continue to do it. Because of the highly technical nature of data processing, new hardware and software products are constantly becoming available.

Over the years we have moved from cards to tape to disk to virtual memory. We have moved from wiring boards to writing programs in 4th generation languages and buying "canned" software packages. We now have $6,000 PCs that sit on our desks and have the computing power that once required a room full of vacuum tubes and several operators. Can anyone believe that these technological changes have not brought about quantum increases in productivity?

This constant increase in "tool power" has glazed our eyes, and has riveted our attention on the marketplace looking for more productivity increases to drop into our laps. Perhaps our industry has finally matured enough to look elsewhere for more and better ways to improve.

Because of this largesse in the marketplace, skills as the other primary component of capability have not had as much emphasis as tools in years past. We have been ignoring something that might have a very significant payoff. Skills can be improved by concentrating on education, broader on-the-job training, and by providing clearer, more consistent practices for the employee to follow. This has been very beneficial in our shop.

Sure, DP departments have always sent our people to classes, but there has been little direction in this effort. One of the problems has been that it takes so much training just to keep up with the new tools we keep bringing in, there has been little time left for education on other things. Our training and education have not been well coordinated with what was going on in the workplace.

There has been increased emphasis on policies practices, methods, standards, and guidelines. If they are too loose, they allow a business to float in the air like a kite, subject to the whim of any little breeze which comes along. If they are too tight, the business might drown. Practices with the proper degree of freedom allow a business enough room to maneuver and be creative without getting bogged down, or floating out of control.

And finally, membership in such organizations as the Quality Assurance Institute and the Software Maintenance Association has been steadily increasing. There are more quality assurance groups in data processing departments. Almost everyone uses a methodology, and has standards and guidelines. And structured design and programming have had a very positive impact on the writing of programs—in quality, in productivity, and in maintainability. The experience we have had in our department bears this out.

2.6 MANAGEMENT—WHAT DO WE DO? _____

Please don't misunderstand this section. This is not intended to be a general management book, but I believe it is important to give a brief explanation of my view of management to put the rest of what I have to say in context.

What does management do? For years business literature has answered this with:

- plan
- organize
- direct
- control
- staff (added relatively recently)

But to answer it better, let's address two other questions first.

What Is Management?

Business literature has defined *management* as getting work done through others, or achieving results through other people.

A few years ago "authorities" on the subject increased the emphasis on "other" people doing the work by stating that managers are not supposed to do any "useful" work. This, of course, is an exaggeration of the fact that managers are not supposed to actually produce or sell the product. Their function is to get the best possible performance from the "other" people who are doing this work. And they may, in fact, work very hard at removing the barriers to their people's performance. But more recently, these same "authorities" have changed their emphasis to flatter organizations, in which managers have to do "useful" work.

What Is A Business Supposed To Do?

The primary purpose for any business to exist is to generate profits. It is logical then to assume that generating profits is a primary responsibility of a manager. Conventional wisdom is that this is best done by providing the highest possible quality product and the best possible client service.

Though departments in large organizations may not perceive that they have direct responsibility for profits, anyone who spends the funds of the business (including receiving a salary) has an impact on those profits. Therefore, they are responsible to provide high-quality products and excellent service to their internal clients, who in turn do the same for their clients, until external clients are reached and treated in this manner.

With this understanding, I can now determine what a manager is supposed to do in my mind.

1. In order to *plan* and *organize* the work to be done, and organize and *direct* the other people who will do the work, the manager must identify what is to be done. To accomplish this the manager must do the following:
   - Play a central role with his or her staff in dealing with the clients to identify what it is that they require to run their businesses.
   - Organize the clients' requirements into related activities.

- Prioritize the activities.
- Assign and schedule the activities, creating a plan.
- Provide direction to the staff to accomplish the plan.
- Mediate differences between the staff and clients.
- Provide a focal point for generating, justifying, and implementing new ideas.

2. To *control* the output of the group, the manager must:
   - Have standards, benchmarks, plans and/or goals to control against.
   - Keep track of what staff members are doing.
   - Keep track of how much of each resource is expended on each project/product.
   - Take corrective action as necessary.
   - Perform administrative duties such as salary planning, results reviews, progress reporting, and so forth.

3. To *staff* the group implies not only selection but development of subordinates as well. This includes:
   - Delegating responsibility and commensurate authority.
   - Coaching and consulting.
   - Seeing that subordinates have interesting, challenging, and meaningful jobs.
   - Modifying jobs to meet the capabilities and needs of the people to the greatest possible extent.
   - Seeing that subordinates get proper training and experiences.
   - Allowing the subordinates the freedom (autonomy) to succeed and/or fail (while controlling the cost of failure).
   - Motivating, influencing, and persuading.

In carrying out the preceding items, the manager should keep in mind two objectives: (1) satisfy client needs, and (2) develop the staff. In the client service function, never forget that it is the client paying the bill. In the staff development function, remember that failure is as good a teacher as success.

3

What We Did

3.1 MOTIVATION—HOW TO GET THERE

Motivation is such a fascinating subject that a number of people have spent their entire lifetimes studying and writing about it. Everyone thinks they know something about it, and I am no exception. Since the software business is nearly totally dependent on human resources, it is a critical input to operating that business. Although I do not intend to produce a major treatise on motivation here, it is a very significant part of the message I am trying to convey because it is a significant part of how we achieved our demonstrated improvements.

While major emphasis was being placed on new tools, the motivational aspect of productivity was given very low priority. Continuing this emphasis on tools, while keeping motivation in the back seat, is like using technical solutions to solve yesterday's problems tomorrow. Furthermore, the cost of hardware has continuously dropped while the cost of people has increased. This is another reason to look at motivation.

Harold S. Longman, the editor of Soundview Executive Book Summaries, made the following comments in a November 1985 letter to his readers:

> Maybe the '80's are the "People Decade." We have suddenly discovered that our great national resource is not our mines, mills and factories, but people. People with ideas, energy, ambition. Creative people. People who are willing to take a chance. People who can be motivated to excel.

This is just one example of the emphasis that business literature is placing on people as our most valuable resource. The strong consensus of the literature, continuing into the 1990s, is that the people must be highly prized.

Like quality and productivity, we took the approach that motivation was too big to tackle as a single concept. Therefore, as we did in the earlier cases, we divided motivation into components as well. These components are **attitude, development, recognition,** and **expectations.** Following are very brief discussions of each of these as we identified them, and as we used them.

Attitude

The most important factor in motivating computer professionals is the first line supervisor. Attitude is contagious, and should be spread through the organization by management. *The cost is zero, and a high positive attitude of employees is the single most effective factor in the success of an organization.* This is management by example!

Blake and Mouton state, "A key link in accounting for higher or lower productivity is the attitudes toward productivity held by the people who work together." They discuss whether the job of managers is to manage attitudes, or behavior, or actions. In the end they conclude, "it remains true that attitudes precede action." They continue, "group norms for productivity and our attitudes toward them regulate a greater part of our work effort or lack of it than we realize."

Over time, the individual attitudes become part of the value system of the group. New members entering the group experience considerable pressure to embrace these values. In fact, people with similar values are attracted to the group, and people with dissimilar values tend to leave the group. Thus, the values of the group tend to be self-perpetuating. We observed that the best people want to get into the best group.

Development

A good attitude without the skills to back it up will only go so far. Employees must be trained to have the capabilities required by their jobs. As professionals become more skillful, they will normally take greater pride in their work, and will be internally motivated to increase their productivity. Thus, increased capability generates increased motivation.

Development comes in three basic flavors: new job assignment, formal training, and conferences and seminars. We were pretty good at changing assignments to broaden employees' experiences—every two to three years in the lower ranks, extending to about double that for the higher levels.

We didn't always do so well in this area, but I was happy to be there and be part of the improvement. In one personnel planning meeting all the managers present agreed that the time had come for "Bob" (his real name) to move on to his next assignment. The disagreement was what that assignment should be. There were two managers who wanted Bob, and both described their assignments as ideal for him. Now everyone in the room—over a dozen of us—lined up and took sides.

By the time lunch came around, we were no closer to a decision than when we started, and everyone was hungry and grouchy. Making a break in the argument, I suggested that Bob's current manager talk to him at lunch, and see which of the two jobs he would prefer. The brief silence was broken by Bob's current manager who agreed that he would do that right now. There were no objections, and Bob selected the job he preferred— a radical departure from tradition!

Over the years more employees have been given assignment choices, and it works very well. The vast majority of people perform better when doing a job they prefer, and most perform better when given the opportunity to participate in selection and design of a work assignment. This is not to imply that employees were asked to choose from all possibilities, but when an employee was qualified for multiple openings, other criteria being met, he or she was frequently consulted.

With respect to formal training, education, conferences, and seminars, we did okay, but we probably should have done more. Monsanto has a generous college tuition reimbursement program, and while we encouraged our staff to get advanced degrees, (and a few did) or to take specific college courses, we probably should have been at least a bit more "pushy."

When we found training, conferences, or seminars that appeared to justify the time and money, we sent appropriate staff members. The same was true when the staff members found items in which they had an interest. But this was "catch-as-catch-can." We had no formal method to help find worthwhile training experiences, nor to record, rate, or share them. But while we could have used improvement here, the scope was very broad, including technical, managerial, and personal improvement experiences.

One significant caution—sending individuals to a class or conference for which they have no ready use when they return is a negative motivator.

Recognition

Even the highest level of internal motivation can be blunted over a period of time by lack of recognition. Recognition should be one of the easiest and most consistent functions managers do, because it is nothing more than paying attention to employees, and telling them when good work has been noticed.

Watch for the good things people do; there will be plenty to note. And there are many ways to demonstrate appreciation: a simple thank you, verbally or in writing, when employees have done something particularly well; or when they have expended significant extra effort. Our customers often note good work by sending a commendation memo. We started putting these on a department bulletin board. We put names in monthly reports, underlined. We gave added responsibility. And we allowed them to participate in decision making.

Much of the benefit of recognition comes from merely taking notice. *A public thank you costs nothing, but is extremely effective in turning motivation up a notch.*

Expectations

Our expectations of others are generally self-fulfilling prophecies. People more often than not accomplish what we expect of them. Expect their best! Motivate them to expect their best!

When a person takes a new job, he or she comes to it with an attitude about work that has been shaped by experiences to that point in his or her life. And having interviewed for the job, the employee brings expectations about it based on the company, department, manager, and other factors.

It is after starting the job that the employee is impacted by development and recognition provided in the new environment. Furthermore, the impact is "averaged" cumulatively with a lifetime of previous experiences. So, the more experiences an employee has had before coming to a particular job, the more difficult it is to affect his or her attitudes and expectations. Consider your own experiences with trying to "change" the attitudes or work habits of some of your older employees, versus "shaping" the attitudes or habits of the younger ones. Remember that part of the job of managing is managing expectations.

According to J. Clifton Williams, in an audio cassette entitled "Motivation for Managers: An Expectancy Model," if there is no desire or no expectancy, or no believability, then there is no motivational force. People who believe they have a chance to succeed will compete. People who do not believe they can do a job may as well be unable to do it. Create high expectations that the desired performance is possible. Create high expectations that such performance will result in rewards that will satisfy the needs of the individual. This will significantly improve the motivational force of a course of action.

Expectations are constantly being formed by the subtle ways behaviors are rewarded and punished. Be consistent. Be sure reward or punishment follows closely the behavior you want to reinforce or reduce.

Knowledge of quantitative expectations is a particularly powerful tool. If the expectation is perceived to be reasonable, this is a very strong positive motivator. The following story makes this point very well.

During the last few years of the nineteenth century, Charles Schwab simultaneously managed two steel mills for Andrew Carnegie, for which he was paid approximately $1,000,000 per year. One day he walked into one of the mills at the end of the first shift and asked the foreman how many heats of steel his shift had produced. (A heat is a big vat full of molten steel.) The foreman answered five, and Mr. Schwab wrote a large "5" on the concrete floor with a piece of chalk.

When the second shift arrived, they asked why there was a "5" written on the floor, and were told that was the number of heats the first shift had produced. Well, the second shift produced six heats that day, and the numbers continued to increase and to be written on the floor for some time to come. Remember, the only investment here was the piece of chalk and a little time.

I don't know what the record turned out to be for heats of steel per shift, but I do know that Charles Schwab became the first president of United States Steel a few years later. *He proved that people will do what is expected of them, if they know what it is, and if they perceive it to be reasonable.* Schwab obviously knew the value of letting people know what is expected of them. We have come to refer to this in our department as the "Schwab Effect."

In *Controlling Software Projects*, Tom DeMarco presents "The Metric Premise," which is: "Rational, competent men and women can work effectively to maximize any single observed indication of success."

This is a pretty fancy alternative way of describing the "Schwab Effect."

At the QAI National Conference, James W. Cush of Metropolitan Insurance told of a similar experience at his company. They began regularly publishing a report of production reruns. The name of the manager with the most reruns during the period was at the top of the list. About one year after inception of this report, *the rerun rate had dropped from 16 percent to 4.4 percent.* This was simply due to publishing this report. They believe this confirms the theory that *awareness will modify behavior.* No one had to tell the project managers to get their jobs off the report. *They just did it!*

In our own shop, the "Schwab Effect" was seen to operate. Early on, we noticed considerable waste in a particular type of disk space. The excess space statistic was published, sorted by manager each month. In less than a year, it went from 47 percent to 15 percent, *by no means other than this publication.* No one was told what to do, but none of the managers wanted their names at the top of the list.

Another story that illustrates the point concerns an experiment performed in the late 1960s by Dr. Robert Rosenthal of Harvard. It was one of over 300 studies he conducted on the power of expectations. This particular experiment was done in a school district in the San Francisco Bay area.

At the beginning of the school year, the administration called in three teachers and told them they had been identified as the three best teachers in the school, and that the 90 best students in the school had also been identified. Then they were told that as a reward for their excellence, they would each be given a class of 30 of these exceptional students.

The only constraint placed on the teachers was that they could not tell anyone they were working with special classes so that the school could not be accused of discrimination. The teachers and administrators all expected to do extremely well under these conditions.

To no one's surprise, at the end of the school year, these three classes led the entire school district in academic achievement. Their average grade level was nearly 90 percent for every subject taught. The teachers were asked back into the administration office and congratulated on their spectacular success.

They said it was easy to do with such bright students, and they were then told that the students had not been identified as the 90 brightest, but had been selected at random. The teachers then decided that these results were achieved because of their outstanding teaching. The administrators then told the teachers about the other part of the experiment. At the beginning of the year, the names of all of the teachers in the school were put in a hat, and their names were the three that were drawn.

In this case, the only difference between these highly successful classes and the rest of the classes in the school was the expectations that the administrators had placed on the teachers, and the expectations the teachers had placed on the students. *In fact, the expectations on the students were totally unspoken, but they obviously had a very dramatic impact!*

There have been a number of programming experiments reported in the literature by people such as Boehm, Weinberg, McClure, and others to identify the effects of expectations. These too corroborate that *even programmers* will do what is expected of them, if they know what that is.

The next area we discuss here is that of **development**, and it covers a lot of ground, generally having to do with assignments, participation, and control.

It is obvious that the assignments given to individuals are extremely important to them, to their career, their education, and their future. What is not quite so obvious is the effect this has on the company they work for. All of us will do a better job at something we enjoy and have an interest in, rather than something we don't enjoy.

Until the last few years, assignments were made primarily on the basis of the available person having the capability to do the job that needs to be filled. Little or no consideration was given to the desires of the individual being considered. Once the decision has been made, the individual was simply informed of his or her new assignment with the confident expectation that the individual would be happy with the new assignment. The story early in this chapter about "Bob" was a major step on the road to changing this approach.

This leads me to the topic of participation. The conventional wisdom of business authors is that we must move toward participative management, and away from the "old style" of management. It has been observed that most of the higher level corporate management today received their management training in the military during World War II and Korea. And that younger people in the work force do not respond well to the "old," dictatorial style.

Hence, the movement toward participation, which gives the employee more of a feeling of belonging and of control. These are extremely important factors in motivation because they help build commitment. *People will put forth more effort to accomplish goals they helped develop rather than those imposed upon them.*

For the most part, there is no perfect solution to any problem. Your employee's solution to any given problem may be just as good as yours. Tell employees what to do, but not how to do it. Give them autonomy, and the freedom to fail. Thomas Edison said, "I know if I fail often enough, in the end I'll just run out of failures, and finally succeed."

Give them responsibility. Let employees write their own goals within the constraints of the work that needs to be done. Don't be guilty of "micro" management. And give them the authority that goes with the responsibility.

The last area to be discussed here is recognition, or reward. One of the more firmly entrenched tenets of behavioral theory is that we all do things because of consequences. And consequences can be either positive (reward), or negative (punishment). On the inside cover of the *One Minute Manager* it says "Help people reach their full potential. Catch them doing something right." We tend to do what is rewarded and avoid what is punished.

Obviously, each employee is different with respect to internal motivation, performance level, need for recognition, and what kind of recognition means most to them. Don't assume that an employee who does a good job every day does not want or need recognition. We all need some amount. If good work goes unrecognized long enough, the employee will get discouraged, motivation will suffer, and quality and/or productivity will drop.

There are countless ways to recognize employees for doing good work. The simplest is to recognize accomplishments verbally and say thank you.

Here are a few final points to keep in mind about the use of recognition. First, the recognition/reward system must be balanced. It can't be all pay and none of the other items. Neither will it work if the pay is insufficient. Second, recognition works best if the consequences are known and definite ahead of time. That is, the recognition is a known target for which to aim. Third, find out what is important to each of your employees so you don't end up giving baseball tickets to the music fanatic, or symphony tickets to the sports fan. And finally, remember that the more experienced people know how much recognition they need (they may think it's none), and have already mastered the art of getting it. But the younger people may be making do without enough, and not know how to improve their situation. Check on them periodically.

3.2 ACTIONS WE TOOK

Referring back to Chapter 1.2, what we had to do first was the research needed to understand our business. We found that we have only four assets that we can control: our people (brains), information (internal and external), our libraries of programs (inventory), and a budget (money) with which to buy equipment and other resources.

Our brains must be used to cover two totally disparate areas of knowledge and information. The first is the technical aspect of data processing. Second, but equally important, is the knowledge of how to run a business. To do either, we must rely on information, either available on the outside, or generated from within.

Information is the necessary glue to hold all of the assets together. If we find we are short of information in our efforts to optimally mix our assets, we must use some of our other assets to make up this shortage. Further, we needed measurements to establish our goals and to evaluate results.

It didn't take much looking or much research before we were convinced that **measurement is the key** to improvements in quality, productivity, performance, motivation—you name it! And since we couldn't measure our output as a whole, we decided to categorize our activities in a number of different ways in the hope of finding methods to measure them. After some experimentation, we decided on the following categorizations of what we do, and why we do it.

What We Do

1. *Enhancements/New Development (small, medium, large)*: These are work requests that have typically been evaluated and approved by the client. They are improvements, extensions, or corrections to an existing system. Preventive maintenance, additional reports, modifications of reports, added or deleted functions, and added or deleted organizations fall into this category.

2. *Emergency Repairs*: Fixing a broken job/system/program/report, and so on. Typically started by a call from Operations that a job has abended, or a call from a client that a report is not correct.

If the client is wrong in the assertion that the report is not correct, this is not an emergency repair—as nothing was repaired. It then falls under the category of consulting.

Typically, these must be completed within two working days, and are a one person-day effort or less. On occasion, operational problems may exceed these norms.

3. *Consulting*: Answer questions of clients and others about jobs, programs, or systems in your area of responsibility, or about general data processing topics. The questions may be asked in person, in writing, or by phone. If a small amount of research is required to answer the question(s), this is also part of the consulting activity.

These are requests for advice, discussion of possible enhancements, reviews of project status, and so on with the owners of a system. Requests from nonowners may be consulting if less than 15 minutes is spent on the subject. Typically, the latter should be referred to the owner of a system, unless previous arrangements have been made with that owner.

4. *Miscellaneous Technical Activities*: These are the little things that don't fit in other categories, such as minor JCL changes, brief investigations, running ad hoc jobs, and so forth.

5. *Evaluations*: This is done when a request is made to do work not falling into one of the preceding categories. Typically, it is preliminary to an enhancement or new development. The intent is to estimate the cost and benefits of the requested work, and to determine when it can be scheduled.

6. *Planning*: Identification and scheduling of tasks to be done, particularly relating to multiple small items, rather than within one of the other categories.

7. *Training and Supervision*: This includes those activities directed at assisting a peer and/or subordinate(s) in accomplishing their work. It may be of a general DP nature (charge to Administrative), or it may be specific to the project or task at hand (charge to appropriate project).

8. *Administrative*: Administrative activities fall into the four subcategories of vacation, education, general administration, and unrelated activities. Education includes formal classes, reading, listening to educational cassettes, attending seminars, conferences, and presentations of new tools. General administration includes such things as attending meetings (nonproject related), filling in time sheets, goals, and so forth.

Unrelated activities include such things as United Way meetings, snow days, illness, personal time, and so forth.

Why We Do It

The following shows the three categories of reasons for doing our work, including examples for each. In some cases, the example could fall into more than one category. You must use your own judgment to select the appropriate category for the work in question.

1. Required by law or policy:
   - Emergency repairs
   - Modifications due to law
   - Modifications due to company or department policy
   - Administrative
2. Tangible Business Benefits:
   - Enhancements
   - Cost-improvement projects
   - Preventive maintenance (could also be intangible)
   - New development
3. Intangible Business Benefits:
   - Consulting
   - Minor miscellaneous client services
   - Evaluations
   - Planning
   - Training and supervision
   - Serving on committees

After getting an initial grasp of our business, we began to subtly alter working conditions in the department, emphasizing the philosophy that system support is a positive, challenging aspect of data processing, rather than the negative, mundane correction of errors.

Since goals and directions must be set within the constraints of a department mission, one of the early efforts we made was to restate our mission and charter.

Department Mission

The department mission is only one sentence: "Provide cost-effective systems to support Monsanto business requirements in a timely manner."

It is made up of four parts.

1. We must provide systems support
2. for Monsanto's business requirements.
3. That support must be cost-effective and
4. provided in a timely manner.

We decided that this mission could best be achieved by striving to operate the organization as though it were a self-sustaining business. We looked toward eventually getting good enough at achieving bottom line dollar results that we could survive if set adrift by Monsanto. This was not the intent, but this approach did create a small business team spirit.

Corroboration of our view that we should be run like a business comes from GUIDE publication GPP-99, "A Management System for the Information Systems Business." "It helps to view I/S as a business operating within a business providing products and services to its customers. With this approach, the I/S business is definable and manageable."

Department Charter

The next step was to write a charter, which follows.

- We must continue to provide "required" services.
- We will anticipate and facilitate business change.
- We will demonstrate that CISS is a major contributor to improved productivity and cost reduction for our users.
- We will demonstrate continually improved productivity within CISS.
- We will demonstrate continually improved quality in both services and products offered by CISS.
- We will be acknowledged as providing the leadership and direction in managing the MIS Support Services function.
- We will be recognized internally and externally as being competent, responsive, and valuable.

To accomplish our mission and achieve the best possible bottom line dollar impact for Monsanto, we determined that our primary objectives must be improved quality of our products and services, and improved productivity of our people.

We also determined from our research and by observation, that there are two approaches to this: people and technology.

What we did in the area of motivation is covered in Chapter 3.1. The conventional wisdom of the motivational researchers is that you can't force productivity: it has to be freely given by the people, but you can make a trade with them if you give them what they want.

Other Early Organizational Changes

Increased emphasis on client service

We felt it was necessary to get our managers, programmers, and analysts closer to their clients. Consequently, we had a small reorganization to accomplish this realignment. We felt this was much more important than keeping each of our groups the same size.

Furthermore, we placed heavy emphasis on service to our clients. Some of the literature (i.e., Martin and McClure) says that one of the more important methods of controlling maintenance costs is to require tighter justification of program and system changes. They also suggest a change review board. In some cases we did this, while in others we did not.

Where there are multiple clients for the same system, we set up a change review board called a steering committee. This committee is, of course, made up of representatives of these clients. They decide what is to be done, and they prioritize it. Our input to this process is to tell the clients the pros, cons, and costs of their requests. *But the final decision is theirs.*

Since we had a charge-back system where we did not have a change review board, we felt comfortable allowing the clients to make these decisions based on cost. They are in a far better position than we are to know how they should spend their money.

We had two rules for our relationships with our clients.

1. The client is always right.
2. When the client is wrong, refer to rule 1.

Surveys that we later conducted showed that our image had improved significantly in the eyes of our clients.

Accountability/Autonomy

Next, we felt that authority must be equivalent to responsibility. We gave this to our people at all levels. Some call it autonomy or accountability, but whatever you call it, it amounts to:

- giving a person a job to do
- letting them do it
- assuming that they know how they are doing
- letting them know they will get the appropriate recognition for the job when it is done, whether it be a pat on the back or a kick in the pants

Then follow through with that recognition.

Part of this accountability is that each individual is responsible for writing his or her own goals within management direction. Some advantages we found of delegating authority and responsibility are:

- It permits decisions to be made more rapidly by those who are closest to the situation.
- It allows the manager's contribution to the organization to be multiplied.
- It demonstrates the manager's confidence in the subordinate.
- Therefore, it helps develop the subordinate.

This also implies some degree of freedom in how the work is done. Everyone learns differently and everyone works differently. There is no best way for everyone for all things for all times. In my own experience, I have used a typewriter for 30 years, as my handwriting is beyond dreadful. Twenty years ago my managers told me that typing was clerical work and I was getting paid too much for that. So, being a good employee, anxious to please my managers, I tried to learn to dictate and to improve my handwriting. To this day, I still do my best thinking at a keyboard. I believed then, and still believe now, that *people should be given as much latitude as possible to work in the manner that is most comfortable and effective for them.*

The summer of my third year in college I hired on as a proofreader for the Quincy (IL) *Herald-Whig,* a newspaper in a smallish midwestern city. My responsibility was to review all of the typeset material destined to go into the newspaper that day, seeking and correcting errors. It was a laborious, eye-straining, intellectually dull-witted job, but one that needed to be done.

One day, sitting in my proofreader's chair under my proofreader's bright light with my proof copy spread in front of me and my proofreader's pencil behind my ear, I looked up to see my boss, in a spate of management by wandering around, coming by to see how I was doing.

Before I knew what was happening, I realized he was barking an order at me. "Get that pencil out from behind your ear," he was commanding me, "and put it in your hand where it belongs." First, I was surprised. Then, as I absorbed what he was saying, I flashed anger. And finally, realizing that the issue wasn't worth turning into an incident, I sullenly removed the offending pencil from behind my ear and placed it in my hand, as bidden.

But I knew in my heart that my boss was wrong. He was wrong, in fact, for two reasons. As a practical matter, the frequency of error incidents was sufficiently low that there was no need to position myself, cat-like, ready to pounce on the next error that occurred. But more importantly, he was wrong philosophically because his responsibility lay not in *how I did my job,* but rather in *whether I was doing it well.*

From that day on, my motivation as a proofreader was considerably diminished.

—RLG

More participation by project managers and staff members

One of the points that came through very frequently in our research was participation. There is a very strong correlation between level of productivity and a feeling of control. If people feel they have no control over their environment, they will not do their best work. Those who feel their input is considered and is therefore a contributing factor in their environment have a much greater probability of being top performers. Observations in our shop bore these facts out.

Employee participation benefits an organization not only from the perspective of improved individual performance, but there is a gold mine of good ideas inside the heads of the staff. A mature and secure management team will welcome good ideas, wherever they come from.

One of the tools we used to stimulate employee participation and contribution was "work effectiveness." This is a particular type of quality circle which is proceduralized by Roy Walters and Associates. It is important to understand that work effectiveness or quality circles are just a means to tap into the employees' potential and need for growth, and not an end in themselves. This added emphasis helped us generate team spirit.

In the article "New Age Management" in *Success* magazine (December 1985), Steve Fishman identified the consensus among business thinkers that management must learn to accept participation over intimidation, human values over technical abilities, and that work should be fun and fulfilling. *We did this.* The management team and the staff had fun! We put a lot of humor on our bulletin board.

But fun and participation require a more mature approach on the part of all concerned. There is a concept called "completed staff work." This is also referred to as "responsible staff action" by G. Michael Durst. The basis of this concept is that the employee takes an assignment through analysis, alternatives, recommendation, planning for implementation, and preparing the paperwork so that the manager can make the final decision.

We emphasized this to our employees. They should be bringing solutions to their managers, not problems. This method of operation has the employee doing what he or she is supposed to do, and leaves the manager time to manage. Another advantage of working this way is that it allows the employee to learn a little bit about the job at the next level. The staff thrived on the additional delegated freedom. In the opinion of our management team, this helped increase the speed of their development to higher levels of competence.

And in some cases, by concentrating on people's strengths, some of the staff got considerable input to their own career moves. According to Peter Drucker, "nothing destroys the spirit of an organization faster than focusing on people's weaknesses."

Would you fire Babe Ruth for striking out over 1,300 times, or General Grant for drinking? *The value of having the right person in the right job cannot be overestimated.*

Emphasis on goals

It is generally accepted that people who write their own goals have more commitment to the goals, and more commitment generally means higher quality and productivity. We told our employees to write their own goals, within the constraints of the department directions.

As part of this emphasis, we recognized our need for more understanding about how goals are set and how they are accomplished. Much of our input in this area came from audio tape presentations by Brian Tracy, Jim Rohn, and Paul Meyer, all of whom are lecturers on motivation. Following are some of their major points that we used.

> The future does not get better by hope, it gets better by plan. Any particular goal you are trying to achieve is a powerful motivator, but the reasons why you want to achieve it are even more powerful. If you had enough reasons, you could do incredible things. When a major goal is accomplished, celebrate.

All three lecturers emphasize that *goals must be written down.* At least two of the three emphasize that *there must be a plan* to accomplish the goals. The goals must be realistic, but not to the point of being less than what we are capable of doing. We must have the desire to achieve our goals, the belief that they are worthwhile, and the confidence that we can achieve them. And we need a list of reasons for accomplishing the goals. These provide the motivation to keep us going when things don't look so good.

And G. Michael Durst, in *Management by Responsibility* makes the distinction between a goal and a wish. For an intention to be a goal, *you must be willing to do what is necessary to accomplish it.*

A key management point is made by these men. When a staff member fails to achieve the agreed-upon results, it may not be the fault of the manager, but neither can the manager abrogate his or her responsibility in the matter. Therefore, it is crucial to the manager and the employee that commitment to goals be obtained. To get that commitment, the goals must be negotiated, realistic, and challenging. *This is a critical success factor,* and it was one of the reasons for the success of our department.

Emphasis on improved communication from the top

We increased the level of communications in a number of ways. We held quarterly meetings of the entire staff. An automated goals reporting system was implemented and has since been replaced by a consistent monthly report format, which includes progress on goals.

We did some formal interviewing of the staff, and some "managing by wandering around." In all of this, we kept in mind that communication is not just sending messages, but also of receiving them. According to Ferdinand Fournies, in *Coaching for*

Improved Work Performance, "communication is a function of thought transmission. *If you make the sounds come out of their mouths then you know the thought had to be in their heads*" (italics added). If it didn't get through one route, we tried another.

Increased emphasis on training and education

We invited the employees to participate in the decisions of what training they wanted, and when it should be scheduled. We observed that sending someone to school to learn something they could not use when they returned was a demotivator.

When it could be arranged, some employees even got a chance to train in their client's environment in order to increase the feeling of belonging. To add flexibility to our training program, we built a self-improvement audio cassette library. It was not used much at first, but borrowings increased with time. We also provided a couple of portable cassette players for those people who did not have one.

We tried to find assignments that were of specific interest to each employee. We believe this improves the individual's opportunity for personal achievement and growth. Obviously, there are limitations in this area, *but we tried.*

Installation of a metrics program

Putting a metrics program in an applications development group takes management commitment. Most of the statistics mean nothing for the first several months they are gathered. It takes months, and sometimes years, to understand the meaning of new metrics. Some of our monthly statistics go back several years, while others are much more recent. *Most of the metrics we captured were automated, and required no effort on the part of the staff. And for the most part, the metrics were captured by the Development Technology group, which was separate from the maintenance groups.*

In *Controlling Software Projects*, Tom DeMarco strongly urges that the estimating function be separated from the development function so that there will be objectivity in the estimating function. The same is true in the metrics function. People will not gather their own metrics objectively.

Several years ago, we developed a change control procedure to be used for updating production programs, and we have retained this statistical information. This information would be much more valuable if we had also kept track of all other production changes, such as JCL, DBDs, PSBs, and so forth; and if, when something was changed, we had identified why it was changed, as new/added/deleted function, enhancement/modification, or error correction.

The first two reasons could be requested by us, the client, or other. The latter could be caused by us, the client, or other. Even with the missing data, however, the information we gathered about program moves to production has been very valuable to our metrics program, and these statistics are reported in the next chapter.

After about a year of gathering statistics about all facets of our business, we started putting a monthly statistics report on the bulletin board. *In many cases, the staff used this information to do a better job!*

Emphasis on quality, excellence, productivity, innovation, and knowing what and how we were doing

We approached all of these from the point of view of adjusting a mind set and expectations. We felt that emphasizing these areas and letting our people know we had high expectations of them would improve their performance. We were not disappointed!

Following are some specific actions we took in our approach to quality and productivity improvement.

- Developed business statistics, which eventually became standards to measure how well we were doing.
- Improved record keeping for our backlog and emergencies.
- Developed standards for COBOL, JCL, documentation, and others.
- Categorized new work and created reporting procedures for measurement.
- Created a Business Practices Handbook.
- Posted humorous motivational materials (e.g., "Herman" posters).
- Selected a quotation of the week.
- Mounted wall hangings on quality, excellence, and innovation.

The Herman posters primarily stress quality, consideration for clients, and responsibility. We developed a file of several hundred quotations (still growing) for our quotation of the week. In addition to the qualities stressed earlier, these also stress innovation, commitment, and humor. Some are interspersed in appropriate places throughout this book. A few more samples follow.

> "I'm sure that other people have had ideas that were similar to mine. The difference is that I have carried mine into action and they have not."—*Nolan Bushnell*

> "The future never just happened. It was always created."—*Will and Ariel Durant*

> "You can't build a reputation on what you are going to do."—*Henry Ford*

> "I am a great believer in luck and I find the harder I work, the more I have of it."
> —*Stephen Leacock*

> "The things that get rewarded get done."—*Michael LeBoeuf*

> "Discovery consists of looking at the same thing as everyone else and thinking something different."—*Roger von Oech*

Christopher Wheeler, VP, Human Resources at 3M Company has said that innovators see opportunities and pursue them with plans that include *"fooling around, making mistakes, being inspired, and failing."* 3M even has a "new venture" career path.

Dr. Frederick Herzberg, Distinguished Professor of Management at the University of Utah, has had much to say about encouraging innovation. Some of his suggestions are paraphrased here.

- Focus employees on the product and the client.
- Encourage unconventional answers.
- Don't force employees to explain and justify themselves.
- Don't overthink. Put some trust in sensuous intuition.
- Enjoy the passion (enthusiasm) that goes with innovation.

We did the things suggested by Wheeler and Herzberg. And we are thoroughly convinced that they are a significant part of the improvements we measured.

Emphasis on humor

We decided that just as much work could get done with a smile as with a frown—and probably more. Much business literature supports this. One example was reported in the July 31, 1985 issue of *MIS Week*. Robert Half International surveyed executives of 100 of the largest corporations in the country. Of the interviewees, 84 percent felt that employees with a sense of humor do a better job than those without. Robert Half later stated that people with a sense of humor tend to be more creative, less rigid, and more willing to consider and embrace new ideas and methods. Our efforts were concentrated on management example, quotations, and asking the staff if they were having fun. Again, *we believe our experiences indicate that having fun increases quality and productivity. We noted a definite reduction in stress in both the staff and the management.*

Humor is a surprisingly controversial topic. There are two fundamental problems with it:

1. Humor differs immensely by individual. One person's guffaw is another person's offensive slapstick. One person's subtle chuckle is another person's "huh?".
2. There seems to be a prevailing belief that, in business, we should check our humor at the door. People say things like "That isn't business-like," and point to an offending humorous item.

It is the latter problem that concerns me most. It is almost as if there is a power struggle between those who believe that humor enlivens all of life, and those who want to squelch it. And sometimes it seems as if the squelchers are winning. I have seen letters to the editor suggesting that

> *Datamation* not carry cartoons, and that other periodicals stop using humorous headlines, when in fact those cartoons and headlines strike me as high points of those journals. And I have seen journals, on occasion, give in to those requests.
>
> So it is both nice and important to see at least one unit of Monsanto, here in this book, accommodating and in fact using humor as a key tool within the business environment. From my point of view, at least, the good guys won a round here!
>
> —RLG

Hiring of co-op employees

For a number of years we have had a co-op program conducted with several universities in the area. Over the years, a substantial number of our permanent employees have come from this group, making this program a great success. After co-op employees have been with us for six to eighteen months, they have had ample time to determine whether this is the environment in which they want to work. And the company has viewed them from the eyes of one to three managers. Hiring of permanent employees in this manner has been universally successful. I don't believe we have made one hiring mistake with this method.

To recap the earlier actions we took, in slightly different terms, *we used communication, participation, opportunity for achievement, recognition, authority commensurate with responsibility, and finally, feedback.* We let them know where they stood. Part of this is the recognition, part of it individual discussions with their managers, and part is simply publishing quantitative business measurements.

Because of the environment at Monsanto, these changes were relatively easy to implement. Monsanto has excellent physical and computing facilities, competitive salary and fringe benefits, and an environment that allows for change and experimentation. In another environment, implementing these changes might be very difficult, if not impossible.

Business Practices Handbook

After getting the earlier changes implemented, we were ready to institutionalize them. To help do this, we published a Business Practices Handbook. This is a compilation of the previous changes and of some of Monsanto's policies and practices. It provides a visible place for us to maintain methods, standards, guidelines, and policies. Following is the table of contents from the handbook.

    I. Mission Statement and Organization

   II. Job Responsibilities

  III. JRA and Goal-Setting Process

    IV. Results Review Process
       A. Sequence of events
       B. Goal evaluation worksheet
       C. Performance summary
       D. Personal development, present position
       E. Performance measurements
       F. Performance indicators
       G. Overall performance rating definitions
    V. Salary Planning Process
    VI. Career Development Process
       A. Sequence of events
       B. Career development form
       C. Career interests
       D. Qualifications
       E. Possible future assignments
       F. Career development plan
    VII. Promotion Process
    VIII. Departmental Procedures
       A. Monthly business reporting model
       B. Categorizing and recording work
       C. CISS accounting policy
       D. Tools
    IX. Business Statistics
    X. Definitions
    XI. Sample Annual Report
    XII. New Employee Postarrival Check List
    XIII. New Employee Sample Work Plan

    The preceding changes helped formulate a more cohesive organization, with increased levels of esprit de corps, commitment, and effort on the part of the individuals. It has provided the following specific, observed benefits for the business unit and its employees.

    1. Management has moved closer to the professionals.
    2. Direction is clearer and more visible to all.
    3. Communications lines have been dramatically shortened.
       • Additional information is being provided.
       • Gaps have been eliminated.
       • More information is coming from the managers rather than the grapevine.
    4. People feel more involved.
    5. People feel they can impact the organization.

6. Management has easier access to the "brain trust" in the organization, and the ideas for improvement this creates.

7. Consistent policies and practices are being fostered.

8. There is increased focus on individual and group goals and directions.

9. There is an intangible feeling that morale is improving.

10. There is an intangible feeling that quality and productivity are improving.

11. Pride in belonging to the organization is being built.

12. Clients and outsiders comment on the improvements.

13. Business statistics help control the business.

Even though our primary emphasis shifted to the environmental issues, we remained observant of what was happening with respect to tools available from any source. The benefits of this approach include some of the motivational items mentioned earlier, plus avoidance of costly and uncontrolled proliferation and/or reinvention of wheels.

Tools Obtained

The following is simply a list of tools we brought into our shop. In the next chapter, measurable accomplishments of our department are discussed. One of the many frustrating facets of measuring is not being able to adequately identify which inputs generated which outputs, and how much impact one input had on any given output. We are convinced, however, that each of these tools contributed to our measured improvement to some degree.

For example, a tool such as PATHVU, which has a definable impact on the ability to measure quality, also probably has an impact on the level of quality, by virtue of the "Schwab Effect" (see Chapter 3.1). But wouldn't it also improve productivity if it improved quality?

In the final analysis, it must be up to the reader to decide which of the tools would be most effective in his or her shop.

1. PATHVU is used to measure complexity and architecture of COBOL programs, and is described in greater detail in Chapter 3.3. This product, originally acquired from Peat Marwick, is now marketed and maintained by XA Systems Corporation.

2. XPEDITER from Application Development Systems, Inc. is used to debug COBOL programs online, and frequently saves significant programmer time.

3. RAMIS is used to simplify report generation; originally from Mathematica Products Group, Inc. of Princeton, NJ, it is now marketed by On-Line Software International.

4. Dial-up terminals allow our programmers to solve production problems from

home, and to do additional work at home at their convenience. (Even with the advent of PCs, more dial-up work is being done than ever before.)

5. Local controllers improved TSO/CMS response time at the office from 1.8 seconds to 0.7 seconds. While this doesn't seem like much, the delay time does impact a fast typist.

6. JAD is the Joint Application Design procedure developed by IBM to improve the requirements definition process. Though the teams that tried it did not get the promised significantly shortened requirements definition phase, they reported far fewer changes later in the development process.

7. We developed an on-line logging facility to monitor emergencies, consultations, and requests for other work, so that we didn't lose track of any of our assignments. As a side benefit, some of what's in this book is available because of the formality brought about by this record-keeping process.

8. Other tools have been developed internally for functions such as data capture and information dissemination.

9. Use of COBOL standards and guidelines have significantly improved the new code being written.

In Capers Jones's book, *Programming Productivity,* he has a section on the impact of tools and environment on software productivity. He shows a comparison of developing and maintaining a specified system in the "best environment," the "average environment," and the "worst environment." He indicates people-months to do the job are 809, 1,428, and 2,066 respectively. That is, average takes 77 percent more resources to do the job than best, and worst takes 155 percent more resources than best. Looked at another way, if you improve your environment from worst to average, productivity will improve by 31%. If the environment is improved from average to best, productivity will go up by 43 percent.

Mr. Jones goes on to briefly describe each of these environments. Since the environment I was working in more nearly approximates the best, that one is included in the following description.

- Integrated text/graphics support for requirements, design, and documentation.
- Good technical library and information access.
- Automated configuration control and project libraries.
- A terminal in each office, and home terminals on request.
- Full repertory of cross-reference, debugging, and formal test library tools.
- Adequate office space with ample storage for listings and manuals.
- Numerous conference rooms for reviews and inspections.
- Automated defect reporting and tracking system.

Later, Mr. Jones cites studies that identified what are called "error-prone" modules, which are responsible for a high percentage of overall maintenance problems.

This is not surprising given the Pareto principle. (That is, "80 percent of the X is caused by 20 percent of the Y." For example, "80 percent of the errors are found in 20 percent of the code," or "80 percent of the execution time is spent in 20 percent of the code.") The studies specified three major causes for the existence of these modules, which are:

1. individual human errors
2. lack of design or specifications
3. size of modules

It is intuitively obvious that the larger a program, the more error-prone it is apt to be. However, it is surprising to me that 500 lines of source code is the limit on manageable size cited. One of the more important guidelines we set for our COBOL code was that it not exceed 2,500 lines per program. Our average increased from 1,372 lines to 1,465 lines from one year to the next, but we made a concerted effort to stay below 2,500 lines per program. *Our data convinced us that no longer creating the very large programs, and in fact, revising some to make them smaller has had a positive effect on our quality and productivity.*

Some Ideas We Tried That Didn't Work

At one point we looked at a more formalized reward system. We considered monthly, quarterly, and annual awards for such categories as best ideas, most revenue generated, and highest percent of time billed. There would be award ceremonies, recognition, and prizes such as monogrammed notebooks, jackets, tickets, dinners for two, and so forth. There would be limits on the frequency with which the same person could win, thereby assuring reasonably broad participation in the awards.

Not all companies have had the same negative experience in setting up reward structures as this Monsanto unit. I have run across all kinds of rewards that have been offered to programmers, especially to maintenance programmers, to thank them for a job well done. The rewards can even be broken into categories:

Trinkets and mementos: stars and pluses to put on paper "plaques," tee-shirts, lunches, dinners, gift certificates, pen sets, departmental newsletter article mentions, tongue-in-cheek titles like "super sleuth of the month."

Career perks: real job titles ("applications support team leader"), advancement on a separate maintenance/technical career path, providing clerical support personnel to offload routine jobs, attendance at seminars and workshops, salary bonuses.

At best, these schemes give the rewarded both the reality and the perception of being valuable. Companies that have succeeded in these efforts have made comments like "our best and brightest are in maintenance" (because the rewards, focused on that area, have drawn top people to the work), and "management gives us autonomy" (meaning "we get to do the work the way it should be done").

But there are some counter-examples. At one company where I did some consulting, a monetary reward system supported those who solved crisis problems. By the time I arrived on the scene, there were two critical new problems caused by this particular reward system:

1. Some problems were allowed to become crises so that their solution would produce a reward.
2. Key personnel were reluctant to train new "crisis solvers" because it would dilute their potential for reward, with the result that a crisis backlog of crisis proportions had arisen!

The message here, I think, is clear. Reward systems can work (Pac Bell, for example, has had great success with very simple rewards presented in a somewhat formal setting with several levels of management present), but care should be taken to ensure that the system is not misused.

—RLG

This sounded like a wonderful idea to the management team. We thought sure it would generate more enthusiasm on the part of the staff, and more striving for these reasonably specific goals. So we asked a number of staff members what they thought of the idea. *The most positive response we got was lack of an objection to the awards.* The majority didn't want anything to do with it! The management team was amazed.

The reasons we were given for not having the awards seemed to be based on lack of trust. With respect to an award for creativity or best idea, we were asked who would decide the winner. We told them the staff would decide, not the management, but they felt there would be prejudice toward friends rather than objective judgment.

With respect to awards for highest percent billed, or for most revenue generated, the objection was that some people were in a job that gave them a huge advantage, and with no additional effort on their part, they would easily win every time. Also, others were in jobs that would not allow them the remotest possibility of winning, no matter how hard they worked. Though we pointed out that this would be a long-term policy, and that people change jobs fairly frequently, the staff was still against the idea.

Furthermore, there was concern that some people might change their work habits without changing their results—just to win an award. And that some might even lie on their time sheets. This was a big disappointment to us.

Early in the game, in the name of consistency, we decided that we would devote one managers' staff meeting each month to reporting standardized business metrics. This was primarily accounting information as there were very few other metrics we had at that time. During the first of these meetings we pondered (argued) mightily over what would be beneficial. We finally settled on graphs of

- expenses

- revenues
- percent of time billed
- analysis of administrative time

We created special forms for all of these and a few others, and another form to report on the progress of "no-bill" (administrative) projects.

At each meeting, each of the five managers presented his or her statistics to the rest of us. For the most part, we were all very bored, but being professionals, we stayed awake. Most of the discussion in these meetings centered around either why one statistic was out of line, or the general format of what we were reporting. Over time, we made some changes to the format.

It turned out that we never hit upon any combination of accounting statistics from which we learned much. Most of the "good" questions, from which we did learn, came from the programmer-related statistics that were being automatically generated by the Development Technology group. We discontinued the reporting meetings in less than a year.

3.3 WHAT WE ACCOMPLISHED

Two things have been accomplished in this department that are of far greater significance than any other items. The first is our feeling of "good health." The research we did, and the contacts we have had with other companies have convinced us that we are in very good shape, environmentally as well as technologically. Our comparisons with other companies convinced us of this.

The management of the department all feel that we have done right by our employees and our company. Furthermore, many employees below the management level have attended conferences and came back feeling the same way. In fact, we believe that *one of the more important benefits of having our employees attend seminars with other companies is to reinforce our feeling of departmental confidence*. It's one thing if your manager tells you how good you have it, but it's another to hear it from people outside of your company.

Our second major accomplishment has been our ability to explain to higher management our contribution to the company. Through the use of analogies and some macro measurements, they now have a much better appreciation of what we do for the company, and the dramatic improvements we have made over the six-year period this book reports on. Though we do not yet have all of the business measurements in place that we would like, we have enough to help us tell our story to people who are not DP professionals.

But in any business function, sooner or later, you have to show that your results flow to the bottom line. After all, the bottom line is the *Bottom Line*. We demonstrated hard results in three areas: quality, productivity, and cost savings. Only late in this process did the quality results "harden." We were able to prove by use of PATHVU that the quality of the COBOL code of our group *improved by 7.6 percent over a one-year period*.

Quality Improvements

PATHVU is a particularly good example of a tool that is a motivator. This was set up in our TOOLBOX with a very user-friendly dialogue. It is quite easy for a programmer to run a quality analysis of a program just written or just modified. It enhances one of the core job dimensions specified by Couger and others—*feedback from the job itself*. No longer did the programmer have to ask the manager how he or she was doing. Quality metrics for the program are easily available at the terminal. And *nobody* wants to see the quality metrics of a program *they* just worked on *get worse*.

When PATHVU was installed in the fifth year of the study, all of our 3,500 COBOL programs were analyzed by the product. In the sixth year, a number of programs were added or deleted to the file. Also, a number of programs still in the file have been modified.

The product identifies two distinct metrics which they use to place each program in a quadrant or sector. These metrics are called *complexity* and *architecture*. The factors included in them follow.

Complexity	Architecture
Deepest nesting level	Number of GO TOs
Level change coefficient	Number of ALTERs
Percent control logic	Excess GOBACK
Number of verbs	Excess fall thrus
	Number of verbs

The mathematical formulation of these factors is the vendor's secret, but in the first instance, just the inclusion of these factors in each of the scores makes sense on the surface. Second, as you will see in a few paragraphs, we validated the scores produced by these analyses through the knowledge and expertise of our senior technical staff, who have the primary responsibility for maintaining the programs we analyzed.

The results of these two scores can be plotted on a rectangular grid. We added a computation which we called the maintainability score, which is simply the distance from the zero point. That is, the maintainability score is the square root of the sum of the squares of the architecture and complexity scores. (Note that a reduction in the maintainability score implies improvement.) Following are these various scores from one year to the next.

Note that the average maintainability score improved 7.6 percent in one year. It can be confidently argued that this represents a 7.6 percent improvement in the quality of our COBOL programs as a whole. The following factors influenced this improvement.

1. The MSA programs were not measured the first year because I didn't know they were there. (MSA is one of our purchased systems.) However, their effect on the overall Year 6 maintainability score is not highly significant as the overall score is

	Average Score				Average Lines of Code
	Complex	Archit	Maintain	No Pgms	
Year 5	104	93	157	3,521	1,372
Year 6	96	92	145	4,482	1,465
Percent change	−7.6%	−1%	−7.6%	+27%	+6.8%
MSA adds	76	109	145	456	1,190
New programs	76	50	100	515	1,500
Deletes				10	
AOB Year 5	190	127	235	174	3,418
AOB Year 6	158	97	191	198	3,246
Percent change	−17%	−24%	−19%	+14%	−5%

the same as the MSA score. But it is interesting that while the size of their programs is smaller than ours, and their complexity is lower, their architecture is significantly worse than ours.

2. A total of 515 programs were added with an average maintainability score that was 36 percent better than the average on the file. This is not a surprise. Some of the older code was written before we had standards, and we already knew the newer programmers were better trained and had better tools than their older counterparts did.

3. AOB maintainability score improved by 19 percent through the active effort of that team. The Automated Order Billing system (AOB) is one of the larger ones built in house. Though this represented only 5 percent of the programs in Year 5, it represented 10 percent of the lines of code.

4. Finally, ten programs were deleted. We do not have the statistics on them, but only ten programs could not have significantly impacted these results.

We believe that these improved results were at least partially achieved *due to our ability to measure with PATHVU*. At a minimum, this knowledge was a very significant input to the changes that were made in the AOB system.

The project team responsible for that system had been trying to sell the improvements to the clients for some time. Being able to show the clients that their system came out on the *bottom* of the PATHVU analysis was a major part of a renewed effort to sell them on the changes our team believed were necessary for the continued reliability of the system.

Running the PATHVU analysis after it had been installed for a year gave us a second benchmark of our code. This was a signal occurrence *as it identified the trend of improved quality*. In addition, we institutionalized the use of PATHVU in our standard move to production procedure. We also created a very user-friendly method for our programmers to identify the metrics of their programs.

The package indicates that the programs we wrote are better than the ones we purchased. And the ones we wrote recently are markedly better than those written in the past. This is corroboration that moving to structured design and programming was a correct action.

It was gratifying for everyone involved to see the quality of our code improve due to improved standards, procedures, and training. But this improvement was in the sixth year, *with no additional emphasis on improved coding.* Now that people can easily identify the metrics of their code, the "Schwab Effect" will take over, accelerating the improvement.

Can you imagine a programmer making a modification or writing a new program without checking the metrics? Can you imagine a programmer waiting for a manager to ask why the metrics got worse, without having the answer ready? This is a giant step in improving the "core job dimension" of feedback from the job.

I was asked by a member of our management what effect this quality improvement had on the bottom line. (This is a very common question around here.) My answer, which seemed to satisfy him somewhat, was "It does have an effect, but I don't know *yet* how much."

What I do know is that our productivity improved demonstrably, and I know the actions we took to effect that improvement, but I don't yet have enough information to know which actions contributed what amount to the whole—or to any specific part, for that matter.

Surely, the improvement in quality must have been part of the reason why productivity improved. I suspect that the final piece of the metrics puzzle will be put in place on the day when we can identify how much each input unit has contributed to each output effect.

We now have the beginning of a handle on a COBOL code quality metric. We have validated the use of the maintainability score by asking our programmers about the predictive value of relative maintainability scores. Our consensus is that it is valid at the macro (total system) level, but only about 70 percent reliable in a one-on-one comparison of individual programs.

At the macro level, if the ABC system has 200 programs, comprised of 200,000 lines of code, and whose average maintainability score per program is 150, its total maintainability score is 30,000. If the XYZ system has 300 programs, comprised of 300,000 lines of code, and whose average maintainability score per program is 50, its total maintainability score is 15,000.

The conclusion we have reached here is that the quality of the XYZ system as a whole is three times as good as that of the ABC system. And while XYZ is 50 percent larger, the native difficulty of maintaining the ABC system would be twice that of the XYZ system.

Though this theory has not yet been fully tested, it appears to our management and our senior technical staff to be very realistic in light of what we know about our current systems, their size, their quality metrics, and the amount of effort required to maintain them.

When comparing specific programs with each other, however, we found that the programmer corroborated the maintainability score only about 70 percent of the time.

This is, if two programs each scored 100, 70 percent of the time the programmers said they were about equal in difficulty. If one program scored 100 and another scored 200, about 70 percent of the time the programmer said the latter would be twice as difficult to modify as the former.

The comments of the programmers, although not as conclusive as the macro-level view, are still a strong indication of the validity of this metric.

From the analyses we have done using the PATHVU metrics, it seems to me that quantification of quality is necessary before changes in level of productivity can be meaningful. Measuring software maintenance has always been doubly difficult for two reasons. First, we could not agree on a unit of production. And second, if we could define such a unit, we would agree that there are significant differences in the degree of difficulty required to install said unit into different programs. It might take ten hours to install a unit in a "bad" program, while the same unit could be installed in a "good" program in one hour.

Is the programmer who takes ten hours to install the unit worse (less efficient or productive) than the programmer who takes one hour? That depends on the quality of the program being modified. And the quality of a given program changes over time. It may be modified carelessly so many times that it gets worse, or it may be significantly revised, such that its quality improves.

And finally, in the area of quality, we saw our batch production abend rate drop from over 5 percent to just over 3 percent in three years—that is, a reliability rate near 97 percent. Is this good or bad? We have interpreted it as good from three perspectives. First, it is definitely improving. Second, with our quantity of maintenance programmers, there were concerns that this ratio might have been much higher. This is a clear indication that most of our efforts went into improvements, rather than repairs. And finally, just having a "benchmark" was comforting.

Productivity Improvements

To talk about the productivity improvements we achieved requires a little background. In the first four years covered by this study, total headcount in our department dropped considerably, while the number of systems, jobs, and programs for which we were responsible increased rapidly. Also significant is the fact that the group stopped doing any major new development. This work was moved from this central department to the decentralized operating units.

In the very early years, we were responsible for the support of approximately 3,668 modules with 56 support people. This includes management and secretarial support, but excludes the 11 people working on new development. That equates to 65 modules supported per person.

We developed so many new jobs, transactions, and programs during that period, that within three years we were down to zero new developers, but we had more than doubled the amount of code that we had to support. But by the end of the fourth year, we were down to 44 people supporting more than double what 56 people had supported at the beginning of the study.

By the end of the fifth year, we were responsible for the support of 9,250 modules with 39 people. This is 237 modules per person—a capacity improvement of 265 percent—which is a 38 percent per year improvement over a four year period!

It is important to note that the development teams were using structured design and coding techniques at the beginning of this study. The PATHVU analysis indicates that the quality of the systems developed during that period was dramatically better than those developed *prior* to the use of these techniques. This is just one more indication that quality and productivity go hand in hand.

This can be seen in the table early in this chapter showing various types of PATHVU scores. Note the maintainability score for Year 6 (all existing programs) was 145. For new programs, it was 100, and for AOB Year 6, the score was 191. AOB was one of the older systems (developed in the mid 1970s), and had one of the worst maintainability scores. Only the most seasoned veterans could maintain this system. However, the systems written in the 1980s had much lower scores and could be maintained by the newest recruits. Here was proof that structured design and coding techniques work!

But what are these improvements worth in bottom-line dollars?

Factoring new development out of the first year's budget leaves $3,400,000 spent on supporting our 3,668 modules. This comes to $927 to support each module. The same calculation at the end of five years was $3,200,000 divided by 9,250 modules, or $346 per module.

If we had no improvement in productivity, and had simply experienced the increases in salaries over that period, the cost to support a module in the fifth year would have been $1,232.

If we multiply this by the number of modules supported in Year 5, the budget would have been $11,400,000. This amount less the actual budget of $3,200,000 is a saving to Monsanto of $8,200,000. **This alone proved our worth to our management,** but we went further.

As a result of giving the staff greatly increased accountability, they generated over $600,000 in savings due to various projects they initiated.

The statistics we generated for the department for the last three years of the study follow:

CISS Statistics

Basics	Year 4	Year 5	Year 6
Programmer-Analysts (P-A)	35	31	31
Management	6	6	5
Secretarial	3	2	2
Total staff size	44	39	38
Expenses, w/o O/H,[a] $MM/year[b]	$3.8	$3.5	$3.2
Overhead, $MM/year	NA	$1.8	$0.8
Total expenses	$3.8	$5.3	$4.0
Number of modules supported	8,950[c]	9,250	9,775
Number of programs supported	4,300	4,950	4,950
MM lines of code	5.4	5.4	5.75

CISS Statistics   (*continued*)

Basics	Year 4	Year 5	Year 6
$MM of inventory @ $25	$135	$135	$144
Average lines per module[d]	604	584	590
Programs moved to production	4,400	5,525	6,760
Compiles/year, batch	40,000	30,163	25,342
Compiles/program/year, batch	9.3	6.1	5.1
Batch processings/year	45,000	43,763	59,864
Abends/year, batch[e]	2,400	1,715	1,971
Contractors/professionals[f]	0.4	0.4	0.2
Systems supported	106	100	90
Jobs supported	2,100	2,250	1,825
On-line programs	1,000	1,200	1,255
Transactions/year (MM)	39.6	45	46.5
Repairs (emergency)	1,400	1,000	977
Enhancements	1,065	1,000	732
Consultations	8,100	11,400	10,377
Staff utilization percent	64.9%	73.8%	69.7%

[a]w/o O/H = without Overhead (the cost of upper management, flowed to all appropriate departments below).

[b]MM = Million.

[c]1 stack of paper 67 feet high, stretches out to 25 miles.

[d]Modules = programs + JCL files + data files.

[e]Abend = abnormal program termination (did not run right).

[f]Professionals = Programmer-Analysts + Managers.

Quality Indicators	Year 4	Year 5	Year 6
Abends/batch production run	0.053	0.039	0.033
Abends/month/production module	0.023	0.015	0.017
Abends/month/programmer-analyst	5.7	4.6	5.3
PATHVU maintainability score	NA	157	145

Productivity Indicators	Year 4	Year 5	Year 6
Modules supported/staff member	203	237	257
Batch processings/P-A[a]	1,286	1,412	1,931
Transactions/year (MM)/P-A	1.13	1.45	1.5
Repairs (emergency)/P-A	40	32	32
Enhancements/P-A	30.4	32.3	23.6
Consultations/professional	198	308	288
Production moves/module	0.5	0.6	0.7
Programs to production/month/P-A	10.5	14.9	18.2
Compiles per P-A, batch	1,150	973	817
Compiles/program moved, batch	9.1	5.5	3.7
Maintenance cost/year/module	$425	$378	$327
$MM inventory/professional	$3.3	$3.6	$4.0

[a]P-A = Programmer-Analyst.

CISS Statistics—Percentage Changes

Basics	Year 4 Year 5	Year 5 Year 6	Year 4 Year 6
Programmer-Analysts (P-A)	−11.4%	0.0%	−11.4%
Management	0.0	−16.7	−16.7
Secretarial	−33.3	0.0	−33.3
Total staff size	−11.4	−2.6	−13.6
Expenses, w/o O/H, $MM/year	−7.9	−8.6	−15.8
Overhead, $MM/year	NA	−44.4	NA
Total expenses	NA	−24.5	NA
Number of modules supported	3.4	5.7	9.2
Number of programs supported	15.1	0.0	15.1
MM lines of code	0.0	6.5	6.5
$MM of inventory @ $25	0.0	6.7	6.7
Average lines per module	−3.3	−1.0	−2.3
Programs moved to production	25.6	22.4	53.6
Compiles/year, batch	−24.6	−16.0	−36.6
Compiles/program/year, batch	−34.4	−16.4	−45.2
Batch processings/year	−2.7	36.8	33.0
Abends/year, batch	−28.5	14.9	−17.9
Contractors/professionals	0.0	−50.0	−50.0
Systems supported	−5.7	−9.0	−14.2
Jobs supported	7.0	−18.9	−13.1
On-line programs	20.0	4.6	25.5
Transactions/year (MM)	13.6	3.3	17.4
Repairs (emergency)	−28.6	−2.3	−30.2
Enhancements	−6.1	−26.8	−31.3
Consultations	40.7	−9.0	28.1
Staff utilization percent	13.7	−5.6	7.4

Quality Indicators			
Abends/batch production run	−26.4	−15.4	−37.7
Abends/month/production module	−34.8	13.3	−26.1
Abends/month/programmer-analyst	−19.3	15.2	−7.0
PATHVU maintainability score	NA	−7.6	NA
Modules supported/staff member	16.7	8.4	26.6
Batch processings/P-A	9.8	36.8	50.2
Transactions/year (MM)/P-A	28.3	3.4	32.7
Repairs (emergency)/P-A	−20.0	0	−20.0
Enhancements/P-A	6.3	−26.9	−22.4
Consultations/professional	55.6	−6.5	45.5
Production moves/module	20.0	16.7	40.0
Programs to production/month/P-A	41.9	22.1	73.3
Compiles per P/A, batch	−15.4	−16.0	−29.0
Compiles/program moved, batch	−40.0	−32.7	−59.3
Maintenance cost/year/module	−11.1	−13.5	−23.1
$MM inventory/professional	9.1	11.1	21.2

3.4 HOW WE EXPLAINED OUR ACCOMPLISHMENTS TO MANAGEMENT _____

The Inquisition

For as long as I can remember, we had a difficult time dealing with higher management. We didn't have that warm, fuzzy feeling that somebody up there trusted us technical types. We had to go through an inquisition for every acquisition.

For some reason, we usually got what we needed, but there was always an uncomfortable feeling about not being able to justify what we wanted. We wondered if management looked at every request in the same light as a kid asking for a new toy. (They certainly did that at the beginning of the PC era, and later with laptop PCs for travelers.) At the same time, we were convinced that the particular "new toy" we were requesting this time was absolutely necessary, and totally justified. We wrote ten-page reports showing incredible quantities of intangible justification. But somehow, we were never able to provide *tangible* justification.

As an example, in the late 1970s when I managed a support group, I began a crusade for funds for dial-up terminals so that the support people could handle night calls from home. The cost of a terminal and modem at that time was about $5,000 for the pair. With depreciable life of five years and the cost of programmers at about $25/hour, a programmer would only have to save three to four hours per month to break even. Furthermore, this would be a great productivity improvement and morale builder for those people who were on 24-hour call.

I could never *prove* the justification prior to using the terminals. Finally, in the early 1980s, we got two of them—just to shut me up—not because management believed the justification! Then the prices had dropped to about $700 per terminal/modem combination, and we kept records to show that everyone who had one was putting in more than the few extra hours necessary to justify them. We got to the point of having terminals in the homes of everyone who needed one, just before the terminals were made obsolete by PCs. But the actual economic justification came after the fact, and we had gone through the *questionable trust zone* one more time.

This is just one of many examples of the kinds of situations which frustrated us and caused us to look for ways to convince management that the things we wanted to do were really beneficial. This was a strong impetus in our effort to find a better way to get our ideas across to management.

The Analogies

Our work on measurements and discovering new ways to explain our needs and our worth to management was partly in response to these frustrations. Since management understands productivity measurements and bottom-line dollars, we put extra emphasis on these areas. And in our case, our management had come up not through data processing, but through manufacturing and plant maintenance, so we slanted our explanations toward these disciplines.

It took a long time to come up with the right perspectives, the right analogies, the right pictures, and the right words to get our ideas across to our management. But they were anxious to learn and were constantly asking questions about what we did, how we did it, and what kinds of problems we had. This was helpful to our cause, as it offered us many opportunities to try out different ways of explaining the answers. When one of us found a combination that worked, we wasted no time passing it on to the others.

I remember one that worked very well. I was asked by one of the directors why we sometimes got to the point of being unwilling to make changes to a system. I asked him if he had ever heard the term *spaghetti code*, and he said yes. I told him it was a lot like a very old electrical circuit box that had been modified by many different electricians over the years. Incidentally, most of them didn't bother to note the changes they made on the wiring diagram.

I asked him what he would do if one of his clients had requested additional electrical service, but the electrician sent to do the job reported that it couldn't be done because of the condition of the circuit box that must be used to serve this client. The wiring had been changed so many times it now looked like spaghetti. The box was so full that the cover could hardly be removed and replaced, and the wiring diagram for this box was not in the file folder it was supposed to be in. (Sound familiar?)

He answered that if the requested service was important enough, he would have the box replaced. And if it was not that important, he would reject the client's request. *Now he understood why we are sometimes unwilling to make modifications to systems!* We then went on for hours in the philosophical debate about the client who insists it is that important, and the condition of the circuit box is not his fault, so he won't pay for the service he needs—*you* gotta pay for it. The director also began to get a taste of why we sometimes have image problems.

The Presentation

After what seemed like several million of these little encounters with the directors, our management team decided that it would make everyone's life easier if we could put together a presentation that would explain to them what we do, and once and for all give them the understanding they needed to direct our efforts without wasting their time and ours with trivial questions.

We began to keep track of these encounters, and keep notes of the ideas that seemed to get through the easiest. My boss and I began to organize this into "the presentation." It took us several months before we were ready.

The first rule of explaining anything, we had to learn, is to know your audience. In our case, the management of our department had come up through the ranks in a chemical manufacturing company, so the presentation was developed to take advantage of this. Since our directors didn't know much about maintaining programs, we had to learn a little about maintaining a chemical plant, so that we could put our explanations into their terms.

The presentation was put together "semiprofessionally." That is, we did not hire outside consultants to do it for us, but we did make computer-generated slides and a prepared text, which was rehearsed very thoroughly. After all, a major objective of making this presentation was to improve our image in the eyes of our higher management. Incidentally, all of the graphics included later in this chapter came from the presentation slides.

We included in the presentation a little *humor*, a lot of *statistics*, and many *analogies*. The latter were relatively easy to develop because chemical manufacturing and data processing are both process based. The analogies were a critical factor in getting our ideas across to the directors. It was essential to put our business into terms familiar to them.

Because most of the directors to whom the presentation was made had no background in data processing, it was necessary to begin with the very basics of where we fit and what we do. They understand that data and/or information comes into the data center, and that it is somehow manipulated to provide the data and/or information required by the clients, but there is little comprehension of who does what along the way. We used the robots in Figure 3-1 to explain the relationships between systems programming, applications programming, and operations.

A computer could be thought of as nothing more than a useless electronic robot. Operations buys these, installs them in the data center, plugs them in the wall, and maintains them. But to this point they are still useless.

To bring that robot (computer) "alive" requires machine programs (an operating system), which allow the robot to accept commands. This is what Systems Programming does. They install the operating system. In a sense, this is the brains and nervous

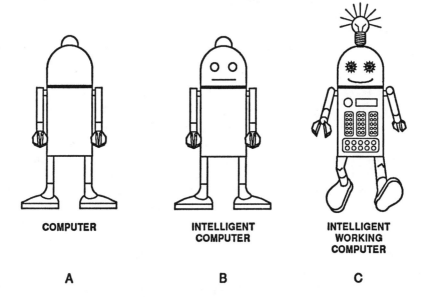

COMPUTER

INTELLIGENT
COMPUTER

INTELLIGENT
WORKING
COMPUTER

A   B   C

Figure 3.1   Maturing of a computer.

system of the robot. It is now capable of doing work, but it hasn't been instructed to do any yet.

Finally, Information Systems (also called Applications Development, and Applications Programming, among other names) enters the picture, and instructs the robot to provide the business information our clients (Monsanto's business units) have requested.

Having explained where Information Systems fits in the data processing organization, the next step was to explain how it provides benefits to the company. To do this requires an understanding of the concept of a program.

This was accomplished by use of the four pictorials in Figure 3-2. Note that the first is a generic conceptual device which somehow combines two or more inputs to make one output. People in the chemical industry had no difficulty understanding it as a *process flow control device.*

The next three pictorials simply show different ways such a conceptual device could be used. If the real device is a pot with heat applied, and the inputs are water and a chicken, it is easy to accept that chicken soup would be the output.

It is likewise easy to accept that water would be the output if hydrogen and oxygen were combined. Then it is just as easy to accept that a program is another kind of process flow control device. It just controls the flow and combination of data rather than material objects.

The point is that a computer program is conceptually no different from any other process flow control device. To further illustrate the point, consider what would be created by the combination of these devices. It could be a chemical process with several steps. It could be an automobile assembly line. Or it could be an information process with several steps. The result of the process could be sent to a client, or it may simply be the input for another process.

The pictorials in Figure 3-3 are of a plastics manufacturing process and a data process. Both are composed of a series of various process flow control devices. The big difference between the two processes is in the instrumentation.

In the plastics process, the engineers could be measuring temperature, pressure, density, viscosity, and so forth, *as it is happening.* Because of the ability to detect variances as they occur, corrective action can be taken at the *earliest* possible time. The action could be to correct quality, productivity, or other problems.

In the data process we don't know what is happening *until it breaks down or the client sees it.* The only "instruments" we have are after-the-fact accounting and client satisfaction. There is no way to detect problems and take corrective action along the way. Once we dump in the raw materials and turn on the process, *it's out of our hands.*

Another thing we told our audience was the dollar amount of corporate assets for which we are responsible. It is not unreasonable for an information systems group to have responsibility for processing of assets several times greater than the assets on the books of the corporation. Consider how many times a dollar flows through payables, receivables, the general ledger, and other accounting systems. Each time a dollar flows through one of these systems, it is our responsibility to see that it is processed accurately, and in a timely manner.

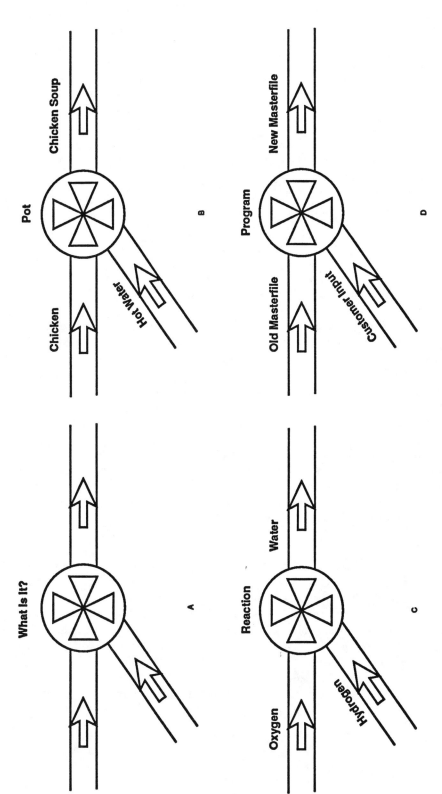

Figure 3.2 Process flow control devices.

Late in our study period, an "inventory" showed that the Central Information Systems group at Monsanto had processing responsibility for over $26,000,000,000 of the corporation's assets. The budget required for support of the processing (not including the processing) was $3,200,000.

This ratio is over 8,100 to 1. It is equivalent to buying a car for $26,000 and paying $3.20 per year to maintain and enhance it—24 hours a day with pick-up and delivery service. Gasoline is extra. But one of the services provided in the $3.20 is finding and installing ways to save gasoline. *Do you know a bargain when you see one? Our management did.* We showed them a picture of that ratio, and it looked something like this.

$26,000,000,000

←$3,200,000

This page would have to be several times as wide as it is to show the true ratio between the line and the dot.

After these introductory slides, which set the tone for the rest of the presentation, we got into the heavy-duty metrics already described in the previous section. The presentation used the same discussion technique as used in that section.

When we got to the point of showing the productivity savings of $8,200,000 per year, there was a brief silence in the room. The department director broke the silence by saying that this level of savings was hard to believe, but he could not find a flaw in our logic. This was the key point in the presentation. We showed what we were worth to the stockholders!

At least partly as a result of this particular point, we were asked to give this presentation to the Corporate Vice-President, Finance, and to several of our major clients. All were very favorably impressed by it.

As you can see from the previous section, the presentation included metrics on how many programs, jobs, and other items were supported, and the cost to reproduce these at the then current estimate of $25 per line of code. The total came to $135,000,000 at that time. This, and metrics such as 11,000 consultations per year, 5,500 production programs changed per year, and 1,000 system enhancements per year are very impressive to people who previously had no idea of what this department does. If nothing else, it provides them with an order of magnitude.

We impressed upon them the need to continue to measure our business. Since we had already shown very tangible results, and since all business people want to be able to measure what they are doing, they were not difficult to convince. We stressed the motivational aspects stated in this book, and told them the stories written here. We also discussed, in much less detail, many of the other points made in this book. Figures 3-4 through 3-7 contain some of the other graphics we used to help make our point.

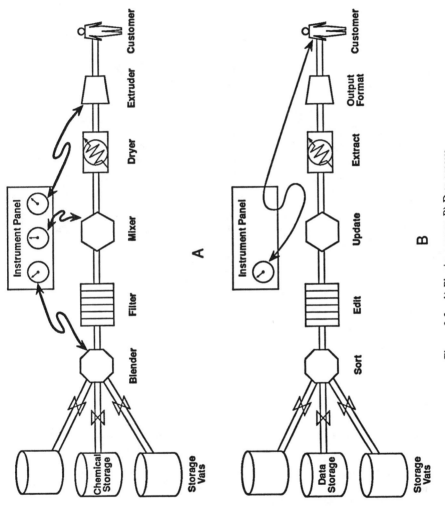

Figure 3.3 A) Plastics process; B) Data process.

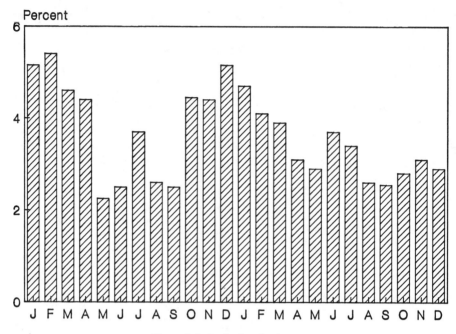

Figure 3.4 Production abend rate.

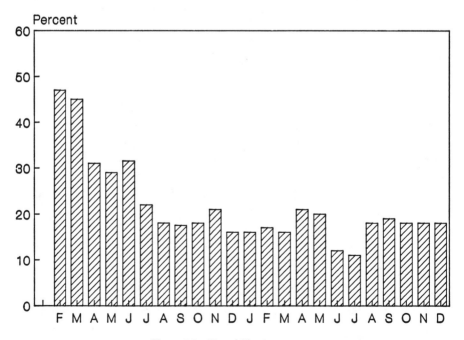

Figure 3.5 Unused librarian space.

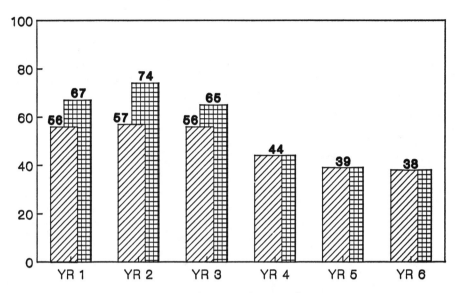

Figure 3.6 CISS headcount trend.

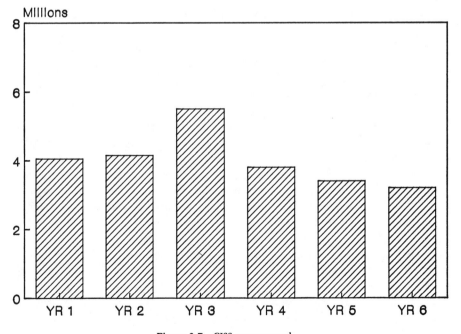

Figure 3.7 CISS expense trend.

4

After We Did It

4.1 A MODEST BEGINNING IN SYSTEMS PROGRAMMING _____

Because of Bob Adams's success in Information Systems, he was asked to do the same job in Systems Programming and was appointed manager of that department. Though I was not moved to that department, I was asked to help him get the metrics started. Of course, we went through a process very similar to that which we had used in Information Systems, but this time it went much faster.

Since I never actually moved into Systems Programming, I cannot report directly on what happened in that department after this change. However, I was deeply involved at the beginning in surveying both the clients and the systems programmers. It is the results of the questionnaires and interviews I report on here. From others I have spoken with, I suspect that at least the client responses which follow are not atypical.

The clients of Systems Programming are largely the applications programmers, though they have some clients in Operations, and even a few who are not in Information Systems at all.

We agreed that the perceptions of the members and clients of the department should be analyzed first. We therefore devised questionnaires to be sent to clients who were too far away to reach, and to be used as a basis for interviews which were held with closer clients and with members of the staff. The objective of these questionnaires and interviews was to find out where the problems were, if any.

Responses from the Clients

Following are the conclusions of the client survey. (SP is Systems Programming.)

1. From 10 percent to 20 percent of the clients were very pleased with the service. However, many wanted better service and better communication from SP, with 29 percent citing service as a problem area.
2. Clients wanted SP to be more visible and/or available, and to be more business-like with 29 percent citing business operations as a problem area.
3. Clients requested a lot of technical improvements with 43 percent wanting some technical function done (but there was no consensus as to what that should be!)
4. The clients believed that asking them what they wanted via the questionnaire implied that SP could/would do something about these requests.

Responses from the Systems Programming Staff

Following are the results of a survey of SP itself.

1. The staff of SP was reasonably satisfied with their jobs.
   - About 75 percent believed they were in the right assignment.
   - A total of 100 percent believed they had at least adequate freedom to do the job.
   - About 88 percent believed their job was important to extremely important.
2. SP internal communications/team work/politics were a problem. The combination of internal communications and internal relationships was mentioned a total of 21 times by 17 different people (43 percent of the staff). The general thrust seemed to be that there were artificial barriers and/or lack of cooperation between the three groups in SP.
3. There were too many unnecessary calls for SP help, resulting in poor service for clients. This issue was mentioned 15 times by 12 people (30 percent of the staff). The general thrust was that they were being unduly interrupted by calls for consulting, many of which were either not in their area of responsibility, simple enough to be answered by someone with far less expertise, or both.
4. There was a concern about organizational structure (who's responsible for what?). This issue was mentioned 13 times by 11 people (28 percent of the staff). The thrust was that people had a need for proper definition and alignment of responsibilities.
5. There was not enough training/education. This issue was mentioned 10 times by 10 people (25 percent of the staff). The primary concern came from the younger staff members, but there was evident support for this at higher levels as well.
6. Communications and relationships with clients needed improvement. This issue was mentioned 12 times by 9 people (23 percent of the staff). The thrust seemed

to be to improve the image of SP and to direct their efforts more toward the needs of the clients.

7. Concern was expressed for running a business and earning a profit. This issue was mentioned 11 times by 8 people (20 percent of the staff). The comments were directed at charging appropriately for their services. I got the impression listening to the comments that the staff believed this action would cause their clients to do a better job of thinking through their requests, and that charging would reduce requests for unnecessary activities. There was even one suggestion that we control our business by use of rates rather than by policies.

8. Management and technical issues kept surfacing. Although these items were mentioned many times by many people, the comments were very diverse. I did not conclude that there was a "consensus" issue lurking under all of the items mentioned.

9. Management feedback needed improvement. Although the overall statistics on "feedback from your manager" looked good, fully 30 percent of the staff felt that the feedback from their supervisor/manager was less than adequate.

10. Alignment of goals with activities was poor. One of the questions asked was if the organization's goals were clear, and if not, how the process could be changed. A number of people said that their goals were clear but did not represent very closely what they did on the job.

11. Career path options were limited. The responses to this question indicated that 35 percent of the staff aspired to a management career path. This is probably more than will be required to fill the management ranks in the future. Furthermore, a number of them at least implied that this was their selection only because the limit on technical advancement was too low.

4.2 ODDS AND ENDS

This section is here to record some interesting observations that do not fit in any of the other sections. They are essentially included as separate minor topics.

Surveys of Users of Standards

If you conduct a survey to find out how many companies have a particular type of standard, after you ask if they have it, ask:

- Is it used?
- What is the benefit to your organization?
- How do you measure that benefit?

All too often, standards are used to adorn a corporate standards manual and the bookcase(s) that hold it, but play no role in the building of product. It is as if the goal for the standards is that they exist rather than that they be used. That is especially true if the standards are voluminous; huge standards make it difficult for the target of the standards to remember and use them, and for the verifiers of standards conformance to do their job in a cost-effective way.

Perception

Perception is reality. We have had many discussions in the last few years about what we should do to improve the environment, and thus improve quality and productivity. Frequently the management would question the staff as to what should be done to improve the environment. When management heard things we didn't like or didn't agree with, we just discounted it. We would make remarks like "that's just an opinion," or "that's not true," or "that's just a perception." But we finally realized that the perceptions are all we had to deal with if we really wanted to impact the environment positively.

If the contractors were sweeping the floors and the staff thought the contractors had all of the creative jobs, we could not just say the staff was wrong. We had to find out why the staff had that perception and change the perception. It might also involve changing the situation, but at a minimum, the perception must be discussed and dealt with.

Temperature is an excellent example of the difference between perception and reality. All of us have been in a room with another person at one time or another when one of us felt comfortable, and the other felt hot or cold. The reality of the situation is the actual temperature in the room. This is a measurable fact. The perception, which is the personal feeling of each person involved, is hot, cold, or comfortable in varying degrees. Changing the temperature will probably change the perceptions, but it might make it better for one, while making it worse for the other. Other alternatives must be considered, such as more or less clothing, or changing locations in the room. It is not necessary in all cases to change the temperature in order to change the perceptions. This concept can be extended by analogy to everyday business situations.

Effects of Lost Computing

The next time we are called upon to give our presentation to management, we will add the following information telling them what the organization would lose without data processing. In the backs of their minds, I am sure they are all aware of this, but an occasional reminder might be helpful to all.

MAJOR EFFECTS OF LOST COMPUTING OR COMMUNICATIONS FOR A FEW DAYS

I. We Could Not:
   A. Accept most orders
   B. Pay bills

   C. Credit receipts to proper accounts
   D. Write payroll checks—wage or salary
   E. Make pension payments
   F. Order certain materials
   G. Close books
II. Potential Nonmonetary Loss Of:
   A. Regulatory compliance
   B. Clients
   C. Vendor good will
   D. Credit rating
   E. Public image
III. Potential Law Suits—Compliance and/or Damages

Future Directions

Following are actions I would like to see taken to help our maintenance programmers and others in the computing function improve the quality and productivity of their work.

1. Automate record keeping of all changes to the production environment, for both hardware and software, and include prose description, magnitude, and reason for the change.
2. Install an on-line "universal" trouble reporting system. All trouble calls, abends, machine, communications, and other problems would be recorded here for later analysis and reporting. All "defects" would be captured.
3. Begin using a 4th generation language for enhancements.
4. Install a testing methodology for all functions.
5. Begin using function points (as follows).
6. Begin prototyping enhancements.
7. Establish a separate "testing" function.

Function Points

I had my first contact with function points at a GUIDE meeting in 1982, some time after I had focused my career on metrics. They were very interesting, rather complicated, and were about the only thing I heard anyone talking about measuring in software. But they were talking about measuring new things as they came in the front door. That was not my concern. I was concerned with the 4,000 programs we already had on the shelf. There did not seem to be any automated way to identify function points in our inventory, and a manual analysis seemed to be an outrageous expense. It still does.

But the world is different now from what it was then. The number of programs has increased to 5,000, and we have a pretty good handle on their quality. It seems that using function points on incoming requests, in conjunction with the quality metrics we have on our existing programs, will help us to better identify the magnitude of incoming work, and our productivity in doing that work. I would like to see function points used on new work.

4.3 SUMMARY

We have covered a lot of ground together in this short book. We have defined some terms, not always using the conventional wisdom of the field; we have talked about actions we took based on our definitions and our experiences; and we have emphasized procedures we tried that worked exceedingly well.

In this section, we look back over the ground we have traveled together to highlight some of the most important findings presented here.

We found it important to focus our efforts on productivity and quality. In order to do that, we had to define those terms in a context that made sense to our people and our enterprise. We chose these definitions:

Productivity = Motivation × Capability (Chapter 2.5)

where

Capability = Skills + Tools
Skills = Experience + Education + Training + Practices
Practices = Policies + Methods + Standards + Guidelines
Motivation = Attitude + Development + Recognition + Expectations
Quality = Functionality + Reliability + Integrity + Efficiency + Maintainability + Ease of Use + Flexibility + Uniqueness + Client Satisfaction (Chapter 2.4)

It is not enough to talk about productivity and quality. There are costs attached to achieving them. In particular, although we frequently talk about quality being free, there is in fact a clearly identifiable cost to achieving it. That cost may be less than the benefits of building a quality product, but the only way to find out if that is so is to measure the cost of quality.

Costs of Quality = Prevention + Appraisal + Failure (Chapter 2.4)

Whatever findings emerged from our studies, it was management that would have to put those findings into practice. It became important to add a definition of management to the others:

Management = Plan + Organize + Direct + Control + Staff (Chapter 2.6)

After defining our terms, it was time to take inventory. We do a lot of what we call "maintenance." What is it and why do we do it?

What We Do = Enhancements/New Development + Emergency Repairs + Consulting + Miscellaneous Technical Activities + Evaluations + Planning + Training + Supervision + Administrative (Chapter 3.2)

Why We Do It = Required by Law or Policy + Tangible Business Benefits + Intangible Business Benefits (Chapter 3.2)

With our definitions in place and our inventory taken, it was time to take action. Here are the actions we took (Chapter 3.2):

1. Wrote a mission statement and a departmental charter.
2. Increased emphasis on client service.
3. Increased worker accountability/authority.
4. Increased bottom-up participation in goal setting.
5. Placed heavy emphasis on goals.
6. Improved top-down communication.
7. Increased emphasis on training and education.
8. Installed a metrics program.
9. Emphasized quality, excellence, productivity, innovation and knowing what and how we were doing, using metrics, a Business Practices Handbook, and motivational displays.
10. Emphasized humor.
11. Hired co-op employees.
12. Obtained tools.

It is easy to talk about starting a metrics program, but it is a lot harder to get down to specifics and do it. Here are the kinds of data we decided to track (from the tables in Chapter 3.3):

- Headcount by task.
- Software inventory, in programs, modules, lines.
- Activities, in compiles, batch runs, abends, transactions, repairs, enhancements, consultations.
- Specific measures (staff utilization, abends/run, abends/month/module, abends/month/programmer, maintainability (via PATHVU), modules supported/programmer, batch runs/programmer, transactions/year/programmer, repairs/programmer, and others).
- Trends of the preceding measures

Inevitably, even in a successful program (and we feel that ours was successful), certain ideas do not work well. Here are some of our less successful endeavors (Chapter 3.2):

- A formalized reward system.
- Reporting of standardized business metrics.

But all-in-all, we believe our program was very successful, as evidenced by the following (Chapter 3.3):

- There was a general organizational feeling of good health.
- We were now able to explain our contribution to higher management.
- Product quality was measurably improved (a 7 percent to 17 percent improvement in maintainability, and a 1 percent to 24 percent improvement in structuredness, over a one-year period).
- Productivity was measurably improved (twice the work load was supported by 78 percent of the people previously used; there was an $8.2 million budgetary savings over a period of three to four years.

It was particularly important that we explain our contribution to higher management (Chapter 3.4). That was done in a presentation using:

- Appropriate analogies.
- Relevant statistics (assets for which IS is responsible, budget and trends for IS, productivity savings, abend rates, headcount trends).
- Humor.

In conclusion, it is important to say that there was no magic in what we did. What we tried, what worked, even what failed—all of those approaches could equally well have been taken in a different setting. Although it is important to tailor what you do and how you do it to your own corporate culture, the message of this book, like that of the 1990s Nike commercial, is "just do it." We hope you find our story useful.

A

Sample Annual Report

FROM: R. M. Adams, CMIS, G.O., G3ED

DATE: cc: CISS Staff

SUBJECT: Annual Report for
CENTRAL INFORMATION SYSTEMS SUPPORT

TO: M. A. Christiansen

The attached CISS Annual Report summarizes the work we did for our customers during the year and the cost of that work. It is a composite of 12 separate Annual Reports compiled for 12 different business functions supported by CISS. These individual reports were sent to a total of nearly 100 of our customers.

R. M. Adams

CENTRAL INFORMATION SYSTEMS SUPPORT (CISS)

ANNUAL REPORT

R. M. Adams

CENTRAL INFORMATION SYSTEMS SUPPORT
ANNUAL REPORT
TABLE OF CONTENTS

I. INTRODUCTION _____

A. Purpose

This report summarizes the year's activities of the Central Information Systems Support section of CMIS.

B. Scope

The scope of this annual report is defined in these dimensions:

1. *CISS Profile:* A representation of the organization and its business activities.
2. *Statistical Results:* Highlight order of magnitude of work performed in terms of dollars, man-days, and volume occurrences.
3. *Narrative:* Brief description of major support accomplishments.

The depth of presentation for the statistical results was limited to the degree of detail required to highlight all significant activities for the year.

C. Source of Data

Data for this report came from Development Technology metrics, the PAC II system, the Backlog system, Emergency system, and from manual recording of various occurrences.

II. MANAGEMENT SUMMARY _____

A. Organization Profile and Metrics

Staff	Monthly average		Staff movement	For the year
Managers	6.25		Promotions, In	4
Professionals	33.50		Promotions, Out	1
Secretaries	2.25		New Hires	5
Co-ops	4.75		Lateral, Out	10
Contractors	12.00		Lateral, In	4
Per Diem	1.00		Terminations	3
Total	59.75		Co-op Terms	10
			Charge-out Rate	96.6%

B. Business Profile and Metrics

	Quantity
Major Business Groups Supported	65
Systems	100
Jobs	2,250
Programs	4,950
All Modules	9,250
Lines of Code	5,400,000
Replacement Cost	$135,000,000
On-line Transactions	45,000,000
Asset Dollar Responsibility	$26,000,000,000

See Glossary (paragraph F in this section) for definition of terms.

C. Business Results and Metrics

	Number of Occurrences	Man-days	Dollars
Emergency Calls	1,000	600	$ 270,000
Consultations	11,000	800	370,000
Miscellaneous Items	200	1,050	560,000
Enhancements	1,000	4,200	2,000,000
Totals	13,200	6,650	$3,200,000
CISS-initiated Cost Savings	33		$ 570,000

Individual Annual Reports include significant additional detail.

See Glossary (paragraph F in this section) for definition of terms.

D. Business Results—Narrative Highlights

1. Procurement
   - Installed vouchering at Queeny, Columbia, and Soda Springs.
   - Reduced vouchering processing cost 30 percent.
   - Completed 23 PCRs (enhancements).
   - Introduced RAMIS for ad hoc reporting.
   - Improved service by staff realignment.
2. MICs
   - Installed Job Cost and remote requisitioning at Chocolate Bayou and Texas City.
   - Installed Preventative Maintenance at Pensacola.
   - Migrated Chocolate Bayou and Texas City processing to Greenville.
   - Installed History Archiving and Job Cost data base purge at all three plants.

3. Order Billing
   * Completed installation of INTOP.
   * Added MIC, Nutritional Chemicals, and Blownware to AOB.
   * Improved batch processing time significantly.
   * Implemented Export Declaration and foreign currency.

4. Payables Management
   * Job streamlining saved $28,000.
   * Installed major modifications to 1099.

5. Accounts Receivable
   * Replaced Accounts Receivable System.

6. Property
   * Decentralized source data entry to 54 remote sites.
   * Implemented Asset Management processing.
   * Compiled Disaster Recovery Plan.

7. Benefits
   * Installed SIP loan feature.
   * Completed PAYSOP conversion.
   * Tested Pension DRP.
   * MIRA modified for new IRS rules.
   * Installed Dental Eligibility.

8. Wage Payroll
   * Added Krummrich and Queeny.
   * Installed interface to MEHI.
   * Data integrity of Personnel Data System improved.

9. Salary Payroll
   * DRP run at Greenville.
   * European data deleted.

10. Corporate Personnel
    * Routine support only.

11. Stock Records
    * Installed stock split function.
    * IRS withholding requirement added.

12. Financial
    * Closing cycle data flow improved.
    * Significant progress on elimination of central keying.
    * Microcomputers installed in Tax Department.
    * Significant progress on replacement of Misco with FSC.

13. Development Technology
    * Implemented metric benchmarks for prior two years.

E. Annual Report Recipients

(Following would be the distribution list by organization.)

F. Glossary—Definition of Terms

1. MAJOR BUSINESS GROUPS SUPPORTED: Any individual plant, operating company, department, or section of a department that is supported by CISS.

2. SYSTEM: A group of computer jobs related in support of a single business function.

3. JOB: Controls the flow of data through a set of programs and/or other modules in batch mode.

4. PROGRAM: Controls combinations and manipulations of specific input data to create specific output data.

5. MODULE: Any set of computer code required to run a job, including programs, subprograms, JCL, data, and utilities.

6. LINES OF CODE: The individual one-line statements which make up all modules.

7. REPLACEMENT COST: This is the amount of money it would cost to rebuild the customer's system from scratch. Industry research indicates this is somewhere between $15 and $50 per line of source code in your system. We have estimated this cost at $25 per line of code.

8. ON-LINE TRANSACTION: Controls the flow of data through a set of programs and/or other modules in conversational mode.

9. ASSET DOLLAR RESPONSIBILITY: This is the dollar value of assets contained within or flowing through the customer's system in one year. For example, the asset dollar responsibility for Property is something in excess of $5 billion. The dollars that flow through AOB are in excess of $3 billion per year.

10. EMERGENCY CALLS: Fixing a broken job/system/program/report, and so on. Typically started by a call to the analyst from Operations that a job has abended, or a call from a customer that a report is not correct.

    If the customer is wrong in the assertion that the report is not correct, this is not an emergency repair as nothing was repaired. It then falls under the category of consulting.

    Typically, these must be completed within two working days, and are one man-day effort or less. On occasion, operational problems may exceed these norms.

11. CONSULTATIONS: Answer questions of customers and others about jobs, programs, or systems in the analyst's area of responsibility, or about general data processing topics. The questions may be asked in person, in writing, or on the phone. If a bit of research is required to answer the question(s), two hours or less, this is also part of consulting.

    These are requests for advice, discussion of possible enhancements, reviews of project status, and so on with the owner of a system. Requests from nonowners may be consulting if less than 15 minutes on the subject. Typically, the latter should be referred to the owner of a system, unless previous arrangements have been made with that owner.

12. MISCELLANEOUS ITEMS: These are the little things that don't fit in other categories, such as minor JCL changes, brief investigations, running ad hoc jobs, and so forth.

13. ENHANCEMENTS: These are work requests that have typically been evaluated and approved by the customer. They are improvements to, extensions to, or corrections of an existing system. Preventive maintenance, additional reports, modifications of reports, added or deleted functions, and added or deleted organizations fall into this category.

B

Sample Client Service Questionnaire

Central Information Systems Support
Service Questionnaire

1. Does the staff cooperate effectively with your department?

	1	2	3	4	5
Comments:	NEVER		SOMETIMES		ALWAYS

2. Does the staff communicate effectively with your department?

	1	2	3	4	5
Comments:	NEVER		SOMETIMES		ALWAYS

3. Do you know whom to contact for information from the staff?

	1	2	3	4	5
Comments:	NEVER		SOMETIMES		ALWAYS

4. Is it easy to reach your contact?

	1	2	3	4	5
Comments:	NEVER		SOMETIMES		ALWAYS

5. Are messages handled in a proper and timely manner?

	1	2	3	4	5
Comments:	NEVER		SOMETIMES		ALWAYS

6. Are your requests handled in a timely manner?

	1	2	3	4	5
Comments:	NEVER		SOMETIMES		ALWAYS

7. Is the staff knowledgeable of data processing?

	1	2	3	4	5
Comments:	NEVER		SOMETIMES		ALWAYS

8. Given the staff contacts assigned to your system(s), are they competent in your functional/business area?

	1	2	3	4	5
Comments:	NEVER		SOMETIMES		ALWAYS

9. If you are using micro/minicomputers, or other office technology, is the staff knowledgeable in this area?

	0	1	2	3	4	5
Comments:	N/A	NEVER		SOMETIMES		ALWAYS

10. Does the staff offer ideas for improvement on their own?

	1	2	3	4	5
Comments:	NEVER		SOMETIMES		ALWAYS

11. How would you rate the amount of red tape involved in your interaction?

	1	2	3	4	5
Comments:	LOW		MEDIUM		HIGH

12. How would you rate the overall quality of the work performed by the staff?

	1	2	3	4	5
Comments:	LOW		MEDIUM		HIGH

13. List any specific problems you have had with the quality or availability of service from the staff, and any recommendations for improvement.

Problem   Recommendation

14. What other improvements would you like to see in the services provided by the staff?

ORGANIZATION: _____   RESPONDENT: _____

DATE: _____

— Bibliography —

ARTHUR, LOWELL JAY, *Measuring Programmer Productivity and Software Quality*. New York: John Wiley & Sons, 1985.

ARTHUR, LOWELL JAY, *Programmer Productivity: Myths, Methods, and Murphology*. New York: John Wiley & Sons, 1983.

Behavioral Sciences Newsletter. Mahwah, NJ: Roy W. Walters & Assoc.

BIEZER, BORIS, *Software System Testing and Quality Assurance*. New York: Van Nostrand Reinhold, 1984.

BLAKE, ROBERT R., AND JANE SRYGLEY MOUTON, *Productivity: The Human Side*. AMACOM, A Division of American Management Associations, 1981.

BLANCHARD, KENNETH, PH.D. AND SPENCER, JOHNSON, M.D., *The One Minute Manager*. New York: William Morrow and Company, Inc., 1982.

BLANCHARD, KENNETH, PH.D., D. W. EDINGTON, AND M. BLANCHARD, *The One Minute Manager Gets Fit*. New York: William Morrow and Company, Inc., 1986. *Success Magazine*, December 1985, book extract.

BOEHM, BARRY W., JOHN R. BROWN, HANS KASPAR, MYRON LIPOW, GORDON J. MACLEOD, AND MICHAEL J. MERRITT, *Characteristics of Software Quality*. Amsterdam: North-Holland Publishing Co., 1978.

BROOKS, FREDERICK P., JR., *The Mythical Man-Month: Essays on Software Engineering*. Reading, MA: Addison-Wesley Publishing Co., 1978.

BURRILL, CLAUDE W., AND LEON W. ELLSWORTH, *Quality Data Processing: The Profit Potential for the 80s* Tenafly, NJ: Burrill-Ellsworth Associates, Inc., 1982

COHEN, WILLIAM A., AND NURIT COHEN, *Top Executive Performance: 11 Keys to Success and Power.* New York: John Wiley & Sons, Inc., Soundview Executive Book Summaries, 1985.

COUGER, J. DANIEL, AND ROBERT A. ZAWACKI, *Motivating and Managing Computer Personnel.* New York: John Wiley & Sons, 1980.

COUGER, J. DANIEL, AND MEL A. COLTER, *Maintenance Programming: Improved Productivity Through Motivation.* Englewood Cliffs, NJ: Prentice-Hall, 1985.

CROSBY, PHILLIP B., *Quality is Free.* New York: McGraw-Hill, 1979.

DEMARCO, TOM, *Controlling Software Projects: Management, Measurement, & Estimation,* New York: Yourdon Press, 1982.

DRUCKER, PETER F., *Managing for Results.* New York: Harper & Row, Soundview Executive Book Summaries, 1985.

DRUCKER, PETER F., *The Practice of Management.* New York: Harper & Row, Soundview Executive Book Summaries, 1985.

DRUCKER, PETER F., *The Effective Executive.* New York: Harper & Row, Soundview Executive Book Summaries, 1985.

DRUCKER, PETER F., An Interview with Soundview Executive Book Summaries, 1985.

DURST, G. MICHAEL, PH.D., *Managing by Responsibility.* Evanston, IL: Center for the Art of Living, 1982.

EDP Productivity Measurement. Orlando, FL: Quality Assurance Institite, 1984.

FOURNIES, FERDINAND F., *Coaching for Improved Work Performance.* New York: Van Nostrand Reinhold Company, 1978.

FISHMAN, STEVE, "New Age Management," *Success Magazine,* (December 1985).

GARFIELD, CHARLES, "Peak Performance," audio cassette. Chicago: Nightingale-Conant Corporation, (708) 647-0300.

GLASS, ROBERT L., *Software Reliability Guidebook.* Englewood Cliffs, NJ: Prentice-Hall, 1979.

GUIDE PUBLICATION GPP-29, *Productivity in the Maintenance Environment.* GUIDE International Corporation, 1978.

GUIDE PUBLICATION GPP-24, *Productivity in the Systems Life Cycle.* GUIDE International Corporation, 1980.

GUIDE PUBLICATION GPP-65, *Measurement of Productivity.* GUIDE International Corporation, 1981.

GUIDE PUBLICATION GPP-88, *The Process of Managing Productivity Improvement.* GUIDE International Corporation, 1982.

GUIDE PUBLICATION GPP-99, *A Management System for the Information Systems Business.* GUIDE International Corporation, 1983.

GUIDE PUBLICATION GPP-117, *Measuring the Effectiveness of Quality Assurance.* GUIDE International Corporation, 1984.

GUIDE PUBLICATION GPP-130, *Maintenance Productivity Improvements Through Matrices and Measurements.* GUIDE International Corporation, 1985.

HILL, JAMES, "The Practical Application of Completed Staff Work," *Supervisory Management,* (June 1980).

Human Potential Magazine, Alexandria, VA.

IACOCCA, LEE, *Iacocca: An Autobiography.* New York: Bantam Books, 1984

JOHNSON, JAMES R., *Managing for Productivity in Data Processing*. Wellesley, MA: Q.E.D. Information Sciences Inc., 1980.

JONES, T. CAPERS, III, *Programming Productivity*. New York: McGraw-Hill, 1986.

JONES, T. CAPERS, III, "Maintenance push is on," *Computerworld*, April 8, 1985.

JURAN, J. M., *Upper Management and Quality* (4th ed.). New York: Juran Institute, Inc., 1982.

KANTER, ROSABETH MOSS, *The Change Masters, Innovation for Productivity in the American Corporation*. New York: Simon and Schuster, 1983.

LEINTZ, BENNET P., AND E. BURTON SWANSON, *Software Maintenance Management*. Reading, MA: Addison-Wesley Publishing Company, 1980.

Management Information Systems Week, New York: Fairchild Publications, July 31, 1985.

MARTIN, JAMES, AND CARMA MCCLURE, *Software Maintenance: The Problem and Its Solutions*. Englewood Cliffs, NJ: Prentice-Hall, 1983.

MARTIN, ROGER J., AND WILMA M. OSBORNE, *Computer Science and Technology, Guidance on Software Maintenance*, NBS Special Publication 500-106, U.S. Department of Commerce, (December 1983).

MEYER, PAUL J., "Power of Goal Setting," Audio Cassette. Waco, TX: SMI International, Inc.

MILLS, HARLAN D., *Software Productivity*. Boston: Little, Brown and Company, 1983.

NAISBITT, JOHN, *Megatrends*. New York: Warner Books, 1982.

ODIORNE, GEORGE S., "Management Decisions by Objectives," Audio Cassette. Waco, TX: Leadership Management Series, SMI International, Inc., 1978.

PARIKH, GIRISH, *Techniques of Program and System Maintenance*. Lincoln: NB: Ethnotech, 1980.

PARIKH, GIRISH, "Software Maintenance: penny wise, program foolish," *Computerworld*, September 23, 1985.

PERRY, WILLIAM E., *Managing Systems Maintenance*. Wellesley, MA: Q.E.D. Information Sciences Inc., 1983.

PERRY, WILLIAM E., *Effective Methods of EDP Quality Assurance*. Wellesley, MA: Q.E.D. Information Sciences Inc., May, 1983.

PERRY, WILLIAM E., Quality Assurance Seminar at Washington University in St. Louis, December 1983.

PETERS, THOMAS J., & ROBERT H. WATERMAN, JR., *In Search of Excellence*. New York: Harper & Row, 1982.

PETERS, THOMAS J., & NANCY AUSTIN, *A Passion for Excellence*. New York: Random House, 1985.

QA QUEST, Orlando, FL: Quality Assurance Institute.

QAI NATIONAL CONFERENCE, Scottsdale, AZ, 1984.

ROHN, E. JAMES, *Success: The Seven Strategies for Wealth & Happiness*. Chicago: Nightingale-Conant Tapes, 1985.

SOUNDVIEW EXECUTIVE BOOK SUMMARIES, Darien, CT.

STEPHENSON, BLAIR Y., PAULA ANN HUGHES, & RICHARD R. HEATH, "A Structured Approach to MIS Productivity Measurement," *Journal of Information Systems Management*, (Fall 1985).

Success Magazine, New York, NY.

TRACY, BRIAN, "Psychology of Achievement," audio cassette. Chicago: Nightingale-Conant Tapes, 1984.

VON OECH, ROGER, *A Whack on the Side of the Head.* New York: Warner Books, 1990.

WAITLY, DENNIS, "The Psychology of Winning," audio cassette. Chicago: Nightingale-Conant Corporation, 1978.

WEINBERG, GERALD, M., *The Psychology of Computer Programming.* New York: Van Nostrand Reinhold Company, 1971.

WILLIAMS, J. CLIFTON, "Motivation for Managers: An Expectancy Model," audio cassette. Waco, TX: Leadership Management Series, SMI International, Inc., 1978.

YOURDON, EDWARD, ED. *Writings of the Revolution.* New York: Yourdon Press, 1982.

Index